# THE PRIESTS AND PEOPLE OF HARVINGTON 1580–2006

## *A History of the Catholic Mission of Harvington, Worcestershire*

David Anthony Higham

GRACEWING

First published in 2006

Gracewing
2 Southern Avenue
Leominster
Herefordshire
HR6 0QF

ISBN 0 85244 019 7
ISBN 978 0 85244 019 3

Typeset by Action Publishing Technology Ltd,
Gloucester GL1 5SR
Printed by
Biddles Ltd, King's Lynn PE30 4LS

# CONTENTS

# ABBREVIATIONS

BAA    Birmingham Archdiocesan Archives
HPA    Harvington Parish Archives
HHA    Harvington Hall Archives
WCRO  Worcestershire County Records Office

# ILLUSTRATIONS

*The photographs on pages 8, 30 and plates 2–8, 13 and 5 are by
Peter Harrington to whom special thanks are due.
Aerial photographs by permission of Simmons Aerofilms Limited.*

# PLATES

# ACKNOWLEDGEMENTS

In compiling this history of the parish in the course of several years, I am indebted to the following for their help: principally to Michael Hodgetts, Historical Director of Harvington Hall, on whose extensive knowledge of its occupants, chapels, and some of the earlier priests I have drawn, and who kindly checked the facts relating to the Hall. I am also grateful to those parishioners who volunteered to record the monumental inscriptions in the churchyard and to Elizabeth Mountford and Margaret James-Moore, who then transferred them, along with parish register data, to disc. The Revd Dr John Sharp helped with access to Harvington papers now in the archdiocesan archives and the Revd John Cox allowed me to consult the registers at St Cassian's, Chaddesley Corbett. Several parishioners and others provided me with anecdotes and photographs, notably Sarah Houle, the Very Revd Paul Chavasse of the Birmingham Oratory, Andrew Ison, Anne Hingley, Merryn and Columb Howell. The County Records Office gave permission for me to reproduce Humphrey Lutley's letter (705:24/633/02). James Quinn and Roger Yardley arranged for the permanent loan of the Silvester Jenks deeds, one of which was transcribed by Shirley McKenna and is included in this history. Sherida Breeden, Manager of Harvington Hall, gave me access to various documents relating to the Hall and the parish, and Abbot Geoffrey Scott of Douai Abbey and Dom Daniel Rees of Downside Abbey were most helpful in tracking down the portrait of Silvester Jenks. Paul Moynahan, Secretary of the Society of St Gregory, Dr James Troy and Dom James Norris of Belmont Abbey provided Mgr Crichton's bibliography, and Mr and Mrs Glendenning of Badge Court invited me to spend an enjoyable evening looking over their beautiful and historic house. Mrs Freda Page also welcomed me to Pleremore. I am very grateful to Patricia Twyman and John Kilroy for reading the text and making useful suggestions, and to my secretary Jean Wilcox who assisted June Hall in preparing the text for publication. Finally, June has patiently typed and re-typed the history, and without her efforts its appearance would have long been delayed.

# INTRODUCTION

Over sixty years ago I visited Harvington Hall in the company of fellow students for the priesthood, and the impression made on that occasion has remained with me ever since. It is a place not easily forgotten and, perhaps, as far as recusant houses go, is unique. This history, however, embraces rather more than the Hall – about which much has already been written; rather, it is the record, as the title makes clear, of the Catholic mission, its priests and people, that has survived and developed on the site after the departure of its patrons, the dismemberment of their estate, and the serious dilapidation of the house.

Today the Catholic presence is centred on the parish of St Mary's, and the Hall, now the property of the Archdiocese of Birmingham, stands fully restored as a precious relic of the faith and constancy of our Catholic ancestors. As such, the building serves to inspire many parish and school groups as well as the numerous visitors who come throughout the year. May St Mary's remind them that the faith is alive and flourishing here today thanks to its priests (one of whom suffered martyrdom) and its loyal people.

David Anthony Higham
Parish Priest 2006

Harvington Hall with the Church, Priest's House and Farm, 1953 (Simmons Aerofilms Limited).

# 1

# THE CATHOLIC FAITH AND HARVINGTON

The small church dedicated to Our Blessed Lady dates from 1825, and is among the group of church buildings erected in the years between the late-eighteenth-century Catholic Relief Acts, and Catholic Emancipation. It represents the fourth and final phase in a series of places of worship associated with Harvington Hall, an important centre for Catholicism throughout the 'Penal Days' when those loyal to the ancient faith of this land were persecuted for clinging to the beliefs of their ancestors.

The Hall, itself of mediaeval origin, was rebuilt in Elizabethan times by Humphrey Pakington (1555–1631). The Pakingtons acquired the manor of Chaddesley Corbett in the early sixteenth century; this then included the Hall at Harvington. As recusants they refused to attend the services of the so-called reformed English Church and, like other neighbouring gentry of the same mind, began to shelter firstly, those priests ordained in the reign of Queen Mary, and from then onwards, the newly-founded Jesuits and other secular priests, particularly those entering the country from abroad. This caused the government to embark on a programme of crippling fines, torture and execution to discourage the continuance or resurgence of Catholicism. It was known to the authorities that one of the old Marian priests, John Felton, had been frequenting the manor house in Chaddesley where Humphrey Pakington's mother was living. Felton was arrested in 1582, and the mission in Harvington may be said to have begun around this time, for Humphrey left the manor house for the more secluded site at Harvington, where he proceeded to have a number of hides constructed for the benefit of the missionary priests. Today Harvington Hall is unique in having the finest surviving series of such places for their concealment, some of which are most certainly the work of Nicholas Owen, a Jesuit laybrother, who was working in recusant houses from 1588 onwards. Owen was eventually captured and died in the Tower of London. Refusing to give away his secrets, his constancy under terrible torture was the saving of many priests' lives and probably the most significant contribution to the future of the whole English mission made at that time. He was canonised in 1970.

Humphrey Pakington died in 1631, but his widow, Abigail, continued to live at the Hall throughout the Civil War, dying in 1657. Her two daughters, Mary and Anne, both made successful marriages, and Mary – whose husband Sir John Yate of Buckland had died about this time – now succeeded her mother as mistress of Harvington. It was she who, in 1677, endowed a fund to support Harvington's secular clergy, financed the priestly studies of a local student, Silvester Jenks, and set up almshouses and apprenticeships on the estate for the benefit of the local people. Lady Yate's charity still provides for indigent widows, but her endowment fund for the Harvington missions is no more.[1]

---

[1] See p. 64 and Appendix III.

# 2

# THE SECRET CHAPELS

Before looking at St Mary's Church it will be of some interest to see what preceded it. Visitors to a number of historic houses will perhaps expect to see an ecclesiastical-looking building or room attached to or part of the Hall. At Harvington it is quite different. If there was ever a chapel in mediaeval times no record of such survives. Instead the precarious situation of Catholics in Elizabethan and Stuart times has given us two secret chapels on the top floor of the house. The chapels were originally approached by a discreet newel staircase, the stencilled pattern on the underside of the treads indicating, so it is said, the route to the worshippers. On the second floor, and leading off from a maze of passages, are the original priests' quarters and nearby a tiny room with a single window. This room is still decorated with a pattern of vertical rows of red and white drops painted on the plasterwork. To anyone acquainted with Catholic theology this could only mean that here the Mass, which is the re-presentation of Christ's sacrifice on Calvary, is offered – the reference being of course to St John's Gospel which mentions the piercing of Christ's side by a lance and the flow of blood and water. On the end wall opposite the window the decoration ceases at a height of about three feet from the floor. Obviously this was almost certainly the site of the altar table, as traces of candle wax on the plaster would also indicate. Was this tiny ill-lit room the first chapel to be used? The intensity of the Elizabethan persecution in the 1580s makes that a possible explanation, but the larger chapel off the nursery a few yards away cannot be much later. This room is fairly spacious and well lit. The brick walls are still decorated with a pattern of vine leaves, lilies and pomegranates springing from vases, emblematic, to Catholics, of Christ, the true vine, and of the love and grace of God given through the celebration of the Mass and Sacraments.

In the left-hand corner of the room is a simple hiding place under the floorboards for concealing the 'massing stuff' or vestments. As we look around the chapel today it is not difficult to imagine the scene throughout the many troubled years of the seventeenth century when the little group of faithful, with Mistress Pakington or later, Lady Mary Yate, knelt before the altar and heard the priest reciting the familiar Latin words of the Mass. The door would be bolted and careful watch kept by the window overlooking the approach to the Hall. At the first sign of the pursuivants the priest would have hastily removed his vestments and taken refuge in one of the hiding places nearby, while all appearances of worship would have been quickly hidden away. There are no such raids recorded at Harvington, but it is known that a neighbouring house at Hindlip belonging to Thomas Habington, a friend of Humphrey Pakington, was searched and priests captured.

With the succession of James I, son of Mary, the Catholic Queen of Scots, some toleration might have been expected. Sadly, the hopes of Catholics were not realised and the desperation of some Midland gentry led to the Gunpowder Plot of 1605. A severe anti-Catholic reaction followed. Fr Garnet, the Jesuit provincial, and Fr Oldcorne, who almost certainly visited Harvington some years previously, were unjustifiably implicated and suffered execution. Fr Edward Oldcorne was beatified in 1929. Under Charles I the penal laws were enforced with less vigour, but the Civil War produced additional problems for Catholics who were by tradition (and ironically) royalist in sympathy. After the Battle of Worcester (3 September 1651) the young king, Charles II, fleeing from the parliamentary army, made his way in disguise towards Staffordshire and passed within a quarter of a mile of Harvington. At Boscobel and Moseley he found hiding places with Catholic families – something that Catholics would remember when the monarchy was restored in 1660.

The reign of Charles II saw the last persecutions of Catholic priests in the frenzied atmosphere of the 'Popish Plot!' The king was seemingly unwilling or unable to curb the instigators of the fictitious intrigue, Titus Oates and his accomplice Bedloe. The martyr priest, St John Wall, who is chiefly associated with the Harvington area, was one of the victims and will be considered at length later.

The inventory of the chapel at this period was compiled by William Harris, who was chaplain at the time of Lady Yate's death in 1696. It gives us an idea of how beautifully furnished it was under the Stuarts and even after the 'Glorious Revolution' had forced the Catholic James II to give way to his Protestant son-in-law, William of Orange.

**Imprimis**                                   **Church Stuff**[1]

One vestment and antependium (altar frontal) of silver stuff with gold flowers; and a white satin embroidered veil.

One white tabby vestment and antependium with gold stuff cross.

One white damask vestment and plain satin veil.

One crimson plush vestment and antependium with silver lace.

One carnation Indian satin vestment and antependium laced with silk lace.

One purple tabby vestment and antependium laced; 4 large and lesser pieces of purple sarsenet.

One purple taffety vestment and antependium with silk and silver lace.

One green tabby vestment with a damask antependium.

One green sarsenet vestment with a green and white antependium.

One black velvet vestment and antependium with a white satin cross with silver and black lace.

One black silk flowered vestment with black and white silk lace.

4 pieces of black sarsenet.

One piece of white sarsenet with silver fringe.

**Linen for the Altar**

4 laced long Altar cloths; 2 plain cloths.

4 little under Altar cloths.

4 for the 2 side tables.

5 Albs, 2 laced and 3 plain; 5 Amices.

2 girdles; 10 Corporals; 6 mundatories; 5 little towels.

4 flaxen Communion towels; 4 diaper towels.

4 little calico strips to cover the cruets.

2 little strips for the stoles.

4 bags for the Chalice; 2 holland handkershose.

**Plate**

2 Chalices and patens; one little Ciborium gilt.

One Thurible; a pair of cruets and basin.

One little box for oils and pyx; one pax.

3 Altar stones; 3 Missals.

The altar stone now in the altar of the restored Georgian Chapel may be one of those listed above, likewise a vellum-bound missal of 1614. None of the vestments from this list have survived, but a ciborium and thurible still in use are probably the ones mentioned here. It has been noted that even at the height of the persecutions, and in prisons, Catholics of those days took it for granted that Mass could not be celebrated without the correct plate and vestments, nor were those items always of the simplest. In gentry houses such as Harvington, only the best was fit for divine worship, and in spite of the enormous difficulties under which they lived they made every effort to maintain a solemn liturgy with the appropriate furnishings, and on occasion, even music.

We must not forget that the Catholics of Harvington included not only the family at the Hall but thirty or so others living round about, some of them employees of course. The churchwardens of Chaddesley noted that Dame Mary Yate and her dependents did not come to church and refused communion with the Church of England. The Harvington mission registers, however, would only appear to commence in 1752. Until the erection of St Mary's Church, burials of Catholics took place (when permitted) in St Cassian's churchyard in Chaddesley Corbett, or, as in the case of the Pakingtons and some of the eighteenth- and early nineteenth-century Harvington priests, in the north aisle chantry chapel of St Nicholas. In that chapel are monuments to the family, and notably the inscription to Lady Mary Yate which aptly records that 'her fortitude was built upon her faith, a rock which no storm could move.' (see Appendix II). The chapel remained the property of the Throckmortons until 1864, when St Cassian's was restored and this area was given to the Anglican parish.[2]

---

[1]   Inventory (1696) BAA, C155. Also BAA C538 Bishop Stonor to Thomas Brockholes at Chillington, 31 Jan 1750/1.

[2]   It is interesting to note that St Cassian's parishioners were still leaving money in their wills to provide lights to burn before the high altar, the chapel of St Nicholas and our Lady's altar, as also 'Mary of Pity' or the Pietà in the early 16th century and even as late as 1545. The last Catholic priest of St Cassian's was John Tory who came to the parish in Mary Tudor's reign in 1556.

# 3

# THE GEORGIAN CHAPEL

At the close of the seventeenth century, Harvington and its estate passed to Lady Mary Yate's granddaughter, also called Mary, who had married Sir Robert Throckmorton. By 1743 times were considered to be sufficiently safe for setting up a more spacious chapel outside the Hall but still within the confines of the moat. A Bill allowing Catholics to worship publicly was passed in 1791, but it was only in 1796 that Richard Cornthwaite, then priest at Harvington, obtained a certificate authorising him to set aside a room for the purpose.[1] The garrets of two cottages were adapted, with the aid of Irish labourers, it is said, so as to form the required room, while the exterior retained its secular character when viewed from across the moat. The chapel was approached from the Hall courtyard and was screened by two parallel brick walls joining the Hall to the chapel, one of which survives. Access was originally by an internal wooden staircase. Inside the chapel is divided into three bays and has a plaster ceiling; an oak altar raised on a step stood at the north end where the present altar stands, and the door at the right of the altar gives access to a tiny sacristy. Another inventory from 1714, largely listing plate, shows what was probably transferred to the new chapel. It included: a silver monstrance for Benediction; a silver lamp and thurible; silver cruets and bason; two chalices (one of them had belonged to Mr Morgan, priest at Harvington in 1700); and an Agnus Dei set in a silver case.

'Upon and belonging to ye Altar' was interestingly a 'statue of Our Lady of silver with sichem wood',[2] a silver pyx in its purse for taking communion to the sick as well as a silver pyx in the tabernacle belonging to Mr Morgan. Lastly, there was a 'case of ye Holy oyls in silver' and a wooden box of relics covered or lined with marbled paper.[3]

Towards the end of the eighteenth century a French diplomat, the Marquis de Bombelles, who was on holiday nearby, twice came over for Mass. Unaccustomed to the practice in England at that time of

The Small Chapel, Harvington Hall.

The Large Chapel, Harvington Hall.

saying the Litany of Loreto and a prayer for George III before the actual Mass, the Marquis remarked that it was the longest low Mass he had ever attended. He was nevertheless impressed by the devotion of the forty-strong congregation and the furnishings of the chapel.[4]

Some of the earliest available figures for Easter Communion as spread over Easter to Whitsuntide are as follows:[5]

| | |
|------|-----|
| 1795 | 54 |
| 1797 | 52 |
| 1804 | 54 |
| 1817 | 51 |
| 1818 | 61 |
| 1819 | 82 |
| 1820 | 90 |
| 1821 | 102 |
| 1822 | 136 |
| 1823 | 112 |

The steady growth is due to the influx of Irish; this is apparent in the statistics provided by J. Brownlow in 1830. However, his remarks some twenty years later show that infrequent attendance and lapsation are not a modern phenomenon.[6]

An old account of the Georgian chapel recalls that its most interesting feature had once been the old altar which, perhaps unknown to some of the priests, had served as a repository for precious relics of the penal days: several small chalices the size of an egg cup and enclosed in a bag, extremely light vestments as used by itinerant missioners, books, including an old register, a long candle, and a curious box half a yard long, a foot deep, clamped and bound with metal. It was apparently Anne Parkes, entrusted in the early part of the nineteenth century with the care of the chapel, who one day caught sight of something glittering through a chink in the panelling when she was dusting the altar.

John Brownlow who took over the Harvington mission in 1824 says that the discovery was made in February of the previous year, but Mr Marsden, the priest then in charge, did not examine the contents before it was too late. A fire broke out about midsummer that same year beginning in the room beneath the chapel, and soon both chapel and altar were in flames. In the process of extinguishing the fire the smouldering heap was thrown into the moat, and when this was emptied some years later, tiny bits of gold lace and a mass of molten metal were found there. Harvington had lost some of its most precious relics – part of its history. However, a missal of 1747, said to have been in regular use from these times still survives, along with the missal of 1614.

The tragedy of the fire of 1823 resulted in the building of St Mary's Church beyond the moat by Sir George Throckmorton, and the conversion of the damaged chapel into the village school. The school remained in occupation until 1913.

It was not until 1986 under Archbishop Couve de Murville that the Georgian Chapel was once again restored for worship. It is now suitably furnished with a late-eighteenth-century altar and communion rails from St Joseph's, Upton-on-Severn. This altar is said to have belonged to a former Jesuit, John Joseph Reeve (1781–1848), who was ordained in 1807 and served in several country-house missions.[7]

Into the altar table is inserted the smoke-blackened stone from the original altar, and above it hangs a seventeenth-century painting of the Blessed Virgin and Child with St Dominic and other saints after Barroccio. The chamber organ brought here recently is by Bishop and is early nineteenth-century. In the sacristy there is a Regency vestment press which probably came from Grafton Manor, Bromsgrove.

Today Mass is offered every Saturday in this chapel, where for almost eighty years Harvington Catholics regularly attended, were baptised, confirmed, quietly married and given their funeral rites. In this modest and plain building the Vicars Apostolic of the Midland District, Talbot, Hornyold, Berington and Milner, the precursors of the restored English hierarchy, came to administer confirmation. [8]

[1] Cornthwaite's predecessor, Vaughan (d. 1792) may have been ill and not bothered and then John Kirk was nominated but did not come. See pp. 44–45.

[2] Sichem near Louvain was celebrated for its centuries' old shrine of Our Lady connected with an ancient oak tree on the hill of Montaigu. In 1694 the tree, already dismembered by relic hunters, was removed and cut into portions from which a number of statuettes were carved and themselves became objects of special veneration. An example survives at Oulton Abbey, Stone, Staffordshire.

[3] Inventory.

[4] Harvington Documents, pp. 6–7. *The Bombelles Diary*, August 1784 'Journal de voyage en Grande Bretagne et en Irelande' (ed.) Jacques Gury, Oxford, 1989.

[5] BAA p. 168, Harvington p. 168/1/1, 168/1/2. Also CRS vol. 17 pp. 363–422.

[6] Brownlow J., Memoranda HPA.

[7] Hodgetts M., St Joseph's, Upton-on-Severn, 1850–2000, pp. 7–9.

[8] Bishop Hornyold came to Harvington on Trinity Sunday 2h May 1771 and

confirmed no less than forty-three persons. He was here again in 1785 when thirty-nine were confirmed. On 11 June 1797 Bishop Berington confirmed eighteen. Bishop Milner came to administer the sacrament in 1805, 1809, 1818.

# 4

# ST MARY'S CHURCH

The Harvington priests continued to live in the Hall until 1838 when Sir Charles Throckmorton built the Priest's House. After the persecution abated the priest moved from the top floor of the Hall to other quarters, (the 1797 inventory suggests North Tower and Withdrawing Room) and he shared the house with other lodgers and servants of the Throckmortons who preferred to live at their houses such as Coughton, Weston and Buckland. From the eighteenth century, therefore, Harvington gradually declined in status, was partly demolished and the remaining buildings allowed to fall into disrepair. However, the church (built at a cost of £900, but elsewhere stated to be £1500) and the Priest's House must have seemed in some way a great step forward. Nevertheless, by 1920 Sir William Throckmorton was stripping the Hall of its remaining important features – the great staircase and panelling – and putting the semi-ruinous building with its estate up for sale. It is due to Mrs Ellen Ryan-Ferris of King's Norton and her great devotion to the English Martyrs that Harvington Hall, along with the church and the Priest's House, are now the property of the Archdiocese of Birmingham. Archbishop Thomas Leighton Williams (1877–1946), a man with a feeling for history and Catholic history in particular, began the long work of restoration which his successors have endeavoured to continue in spite of rising costs.

A considerable amount of more recent work is due to another historian whose interests have extended to the arts, Archbishop Maurice Couve de Murville, who retired in 1999.

It is, therefore, a tribute to the wholehearted involvement of the Archdiocese that Harvington and its Hall stand today as the shrine of the Midland Martyrs and a place of pilgrimage for all the parishes and schools of the diocese. After Stonor, Harvington is the next oldest Mission in the Midlands and one of the oldest in the whole of England.

## DESCRIPTION OF THE CHURCH

St Mary's was built in the reign of George IV. Two estimates and a plan have survived.[1] The first, dated 27 May 1822 was provided by J Watts, a builder of Alcester, and quoted the sum of £327 10s 0d. The second estimate from Joseph Guest of the Masons Arms, Dudley, is undated but provides the following information:

> Harvington Chapel: to find Masons work, Carpenters Ditto Smiths work, Lime & Stone getting, sand getting (sic) Glaziers work with best glass, two coats of Plastering on Ceiling and Walls
> Boarded floor and best Slating for Roof covering, Chapel 54 foot by 24 Do in the clear, 20 foot high from the bottom of the foundation to the wall plates, you to find carriage of Materials whatever to the Building and Timber of all dimentions (sic) for the same and all the Bricks and Tiles in the old Barn, and you to allow five pounds to pull down the old Barn and clean the Bricks and Tiles for use. Vestry and Porch 10 foot by 12 Do for the sum of £257 –

The plan and drawing accompanying these estimates is not dated or signed. It shows a building similar to that which exists today but without the few improvements of the final design. It is nevertheless rustic in appearance and the Y-shaped painted wooden tracery is typical of its period.

Of local red sandstone the original church consisted of nave and sanctuary, to which a large battlemented porch or narthex and sacristy were added in 1854. Behind the font is a stained-glass window by Hardman of Birmingham given in 2005 in memory of Ann Mulroy. It depicts St Anne with the Blessed Virgin, St Margaret Clitherow, St Nicholas Owen and Cardinal Newman. A recess in this spacious area formerly occupied by a Calvary group was made into a shrine of St John Wall in 1987. A bronze plaque by Faith Tolkien, daughter of the writer J R Tolkien, represents the martyr, whose association with the Harvington area is conveyed by a scene incorporating as background the Hall and its waterfowl, sheep, and an apple tree typical of Worcestershire. The priest is depicted wearing the ordinary clothes of the period and standing within an arched frame ornamented with wheat and grapes, symbolic of the Mass which he celebrated in secret for his people. The votive light stand and bracket are the work of a local craftsman and parishioner, Frank Verlic. The wooden railings in front came from Osgodby, an old Catholic house in Lincolnshire, now demolished.

St Mary's Church: the interior, c.1875.

In 1888 the whole church was re-decorated according to contemporary taste. The sanctuary walls were covered with a heavy diaper pattern in crimson and gold, and the roof had roundels of angel musicians (now restored.) The rest of the building was adorned with representations of prophets and Marian emblems. The blank window nearest the gallery was filled with a painting of the Visitation of Our Lady by Robert Hopkins of Abergavenny, who also designed and supervised the other murals. Finally, a wrought-iron screen surmounted by a gilded cross was erected in the sanctuary. The whole scheme merited an enthusiastic notice in *The Tablet* of that date,[2] but fashions change, and many years later the building once more reverted to a simpler decoration.

In the wake of the Second Vatican Council, the old altar was replaced by a freestanding altar table of white marble, the supporting pedestal incorporating a terracotta sculpture of the Pietà by a Maltese artist, Carmel Cauchi. This sculpture is now only visible on Good Friday, an appropriate occasion, since the altar is normally covered with an embroidered red velvet frontal which came from the former convent of English Benedictine nuns in Brussels and was made for Abbess Mary Vavasour's Golden Jubilee of Profession in 1678. The reredos now incorporates finely carved tabernacle doors from the eighteenth century.

The east window was filled with new stained glass by John Hardman and Son in 1893. Given by Annie Spink in memory of her late husband, Charles Austin Spink, it includes Our Lady, enthroned with the Holy Child, and grouped around them the patron saints of the Hailes and Spink family: St Charles Borromeo, St Augustine, St Joseph, St Edward the Confessor, St Anne and St Elizabeth of Hungary. The small lights have angels and the centre one the Holy Spirit in the form of a Dove.[3] Sixty years later Mrs Watts of Sion House provided three other panels in memory of her husband, Humphrey Watts: in the centre is St Thomas More, on the right the Carthusian martyr, St Humphrey Middlemore, whose family came from Edgbaston, and on the left St John Fisher and the Franciscan, St John Wall. Finally, in the 1970s the three bottom panels, consisting of a rose and fleur-de-lys, were added by Father Joseph Lacy and Mrs Janet Arbuthnott. It was also through the generosity of Mrs Watts that the sanctuary was panelled in 1949, the woodwork providing a suitable contrast to the gilded candlesticks which are a memorial to Gordon and Mary Winifred Higham.

Looking towards the west door and on the right side of the church

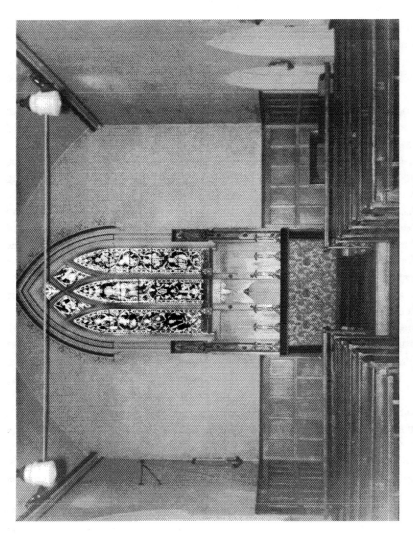

St Mary's Church: the interior, 1954.

are further memorials. The stained-glass window near the eagle lectern was given by Mrs Watts in 1920 in thanksgiving for the safe return of her two sons from the First World War. The window depicts the archangels Michael and Raphael, to whom the Bible attributes defence and healing, together with other angels. The monuments on the wall are to two of the Trafford family, local Catholic landowners, who lived nearby at the house called Pleremore. William Trafford died young in 1829 and his son, also William, in 1901. The Trafford vault lies between the two windows nearest the west end. The left-hand wall of the building as seen from the sanctuary has a noticeable slope and two blocked windows. Not long after its construction it was found necessary to insert tie rods (11 June, 1828) and eventually to shore up this wall by building the Priest's House against it. The blocked window nearest the altar is now filled by statue of St John Wall, the Harvington martyr. The figure, in bronze resin, is the work of Gabrielle Mewburn Mercer, sculptor and daughter of the London sculptor Thomas Mewburn Crook. Around the walls are the consecration crosses incised in stone (the consecration only took place in 1985) and the carved wood Stations of the Cross.

[1] WCRO DRS/1557.

[2] *The Tablet*, Saturday, 8 December, 1888.

[3] Fr Harris said that Mrs Spink thought the work could be done for £50, did not see her way to paying £100, but thought she might stretch a point to £75. She wished it to be highly coloured, and no extras.

## THE ORGAN

Until the 1888 re-decoration the church only possessed an harmonium. In that year it was replaced by an organ from the Catholic church in Stourbridge. The Harvington organ is one of the few surviving instruments built by Henry Cephas Lincoln of Holborn, London. Henry, whose father John was also an organ builder, had been apprenticed to another London firm, Flight and Robson, joined his father in the business in 1810.[1] An organ built by them in 1814 had the nameplate 'Lincoln & Son', but the elder Lincoln must have died or retired shortly afterwards, for by 1819 the name plates only mention Henry. Lincoln remained in business for another couple of decades, but failed to complete an important organ for St Olave's, Southwark, after which nothing more is heard of him. It is said that he died in 1864.

The organ now in St Mary's was originally designed for St Austin's Catholic Chapel (as it was then called) in Stafford at the cost of 'about £250 and upwards'. Rather curiously the instrument was purchased without a case and a local joiner, a Mr Smith, was engaged to make one. The case survives to this day, and although a somewhat rustic affair, is not without a certain interest.

Possibly St Austin's was short of funds at this time, although Thomas Price, its priest, soon bought another organ and moved his first purchase to the school. After some minor alterations Price then proceeded to sell it in 1822 to John Brownlow who was keen to have an organ for his recently built chapel in Stourbridge. Mr Smith was apparently responsible for negotiating the sale, dismantling it and re-erecting it in Stourbridge. Brownlow paid £150 for his acquisition. Price wrote to Brownlow as follows:

My dear Sir

I hope the organ will arrive safe, & when put in yr. Chapel, will entirely meet your approbation. All I can say is, that I think you have got a most excellent bargain, & I think that I may claim to myself, without vanity some judgement in musical Instruments. The whole experience of this organ, with the addition of the new Case & other improvements wh. Mr. Smith has added since it was down in the school, has laid me upwards of £260. So much for London & Lincoln! It was not out of any avaritious (sic) motive that I wished to keep up to the price mentioned, when I last saw you, but I must be satisfied I suppose, with the bargain that Mr. Smith has made, & do not mean to recede from it. Any Money that you can send back by Mr. Smith in part of payment will be highly accept-able to some of my Duns ...

I shall be happy at any time to see you & believe me sincerely yrs.

      St Austins        Thos. Price

      Sunday night

Mrs. Frith begs her respects.[2]

When Fr Harris re-decorated St Mary's in 1888 he managed to replace its harmonium with what *The Tablet* then described as this 'sweet toned organ' from Stourbridge, an addition that would surely have delighted his predecessor, John Brownlow.

The Harvington organ exactly fits the description in the invoice of 1819; moreover, on the batten above the keyboard it bears the name of Henry Cephas Lincoln 'Maker to the Prince Regent'. The words which are now difficult to decipher refer to Lincoln's commission to build an organ for His Royal Highness in the Pavilion at Brighton.

During its 113 years in Harvington the instrument has inevitably undergone various alterations. To begin with it was both a finger and a barrel organ, capable of supplying certain accompaniments if, by chance, no player was available. In fact its three barrels could provide the following items, all of them indicative of the kind of music sung in Catholic churches and chapels in the late-eighteenth and early-nineteenth centuries – in many respects, it would seem, far more liturgically correct than the music heard in many of our churches today.

1st Barrel: Asperges and Dumont's Gregorian Mass. 2nd Barrel: The same Asperges over again and the Gregorian Missa de Angelis. 3rd Barrel: the following hymns:

1. O Salutaris Hostia by Webbe.
2. Tantum ergo in D Majr. by Do.
3. Stabat Mater by Do.  .
4. Adeste fideles by Do.
5. Veni Creator Spiritus by Novello.
6. Regina Coeli by Webbe.
7. Veni Sancte Spiritus by Do.
8. Tantum ergo, in 3 by Do.
9. O Filii et filiae by Do.
10. Hymn at Vespers for Sts. Peter & Paul by Do.

Unfortunately, from an antiquarian viewpoint, the barrel mechanism was removed in more recent times, but it is hoped to rectify other unsympathetic alterations when it becomes possible to carry out a thorough restoration.

The specification is currently as follows:

Manual CC-f 54 notes
Open Diapason 8 ft from Bottom g up, bottom 7 notes wood
Stopt Diapason 8ft Full Compas
Principal 4ft
Fifteenth 2ft
Sesquiatera 3 rks Notes 1–24
Cornet 3 rks Notes 25–54
Pedal CCC-f 30 Notes (added in 1920s)
Bourdon 16ft

¹ Lincoln's father is mentioned in the Diary of William Mawhood, woollen draper of Finchley, friend of Bishop Challoner, and embassy chapel organist.
² HPA The Mrs Frith, who is mentioned in the letter, was a wealthy benefactress of the Stafford mission. cf Staffordshire Catholic History No 14.1974.
³ 'De Angelis on the Barrel organ 1819,' Michael Hodgetts.
  *Midland Catholic History* I (1991) pp. 44–6.

# 5

# THE PRIEST'S HOUSE

A church (or as it was called at the time 'chapel') had, at last, been erected in 1825; it was now time for special provision to be made for the priests, who had lived in rooms in the Hall for more than two hundred years. The Priest's House was begun in 1837 by Sir Charles Throckmorton at the cost of £800 and completed the following year. Father Brownlow records that on 5 October 1838 'I entered the said new House, as my future place of residence. It had been built where it stands, to strengthen the Chapel; the walls of the church had given way, particularly on that side.' Not surprisingly this late Georgian-style building, as seen from the east, overshadows the little church and was known by one parish priest as 'the lighthouse', but from the front of the church it almost disappears.

When Dom Bede Camm came here in the 1900s he described the house as 'embowered in a walled garden teeming with fruit trees', and so it remains today, with the extensive brick walls of the Elizabethan Great Garden enclosing it and stretching beyond to include what is now the car park.[1] Humphrey Pakington had a passion for gardening and it was an interest shared by his widow and daughter, Anne, who married Sir Henry Audley of Berechurch, Essex. Writing to her mother in the 1630s, Anne hoped to obtain for her certain unusual flowers, but her husband, Sir Henry, was also instrumental in securing fruit trees for Harvington, which would have been planted in the Great Garden. A probable survivor from this garden is the very rare medicinal herb known as 'Birthwort' (*Aristolockia Clemetitis*) commonly used to speed up labour and principally found in nunneries where the nuns had midwifery duties. At Harvington it romps away.

We have some idea of the furnishings of the house because Brownlow compiled a list of his own possessions in 1857. Taking them room-by-room, we know that, for instance, the furniture was on the

The Priest's House, *c.*1920.

whole simple painted deal, the more quality pieces having been
provided by the Throckmortons and brought over from the Hall, to
which they have now returned. The kitchen had the customary iron
range and was fitted up with built-in cupboards which still exist. From
the kitchen a flight of steps leads down to the dairy and wine cellar,
where formerly stood the barrels and earthenware crocks, together
with 'all the bottles with their contents, except 3 doz. of Sir Robts
(Throckmorton) and the Altar Wine.'

The Brewhouse and the Pigeon House are mentioned, but seemingly
Brownlow quickly tired of the pigeons and their mess; instead the
pigeons were replaced by garden implements, while the brewhouse was
also home to a variety of useful items such as a bed warming pan.[2]

The Parlour (the nomenclature is reminiscent of earlier times)
which is now the Priest's study was furnished with chairs, a clock
under a glass cover, a case of stuffed birds, a picture in a gilded
frame, books, and a silk umbrella. Above the parlour in what is now
the principal bedroom there was more painted deal furniture, but also
the accoutrements of a country priest, 'All the Guns in the House with
their appurtenances, powder, shot'. The other two bedrooms had the
usual pieces of furniture, but one of them actually possessed
mahogany four poster bedsteads, one of which appears to have
survived down to modern times. The remaining top floor was desig-

nated the Library and is now the parish office. It has floor to ceiling cupboards and once had a mahogany bureau, a couple of writing desks, minerals and fossils, a view of Caverswall Castle and curiously a 'small portrait of good little Pain.'[3]

[1] Dom Bede Camm, O.S.B., *Forgotten Shrines*, London, Macdonald & Evans, pp. 253–74, 1910.

[2] The Pigeon House was adjacent to the Brewhouse which is now called 'The Stable', a parish room. A timber-framed dovecote also formerly stood on the site of the church heating chamber. This latter has been demolished. (Hodgkinson 1943, reprint of *Recent Discoveries at Harvington Hall*, Birmingham Archaeological Society Transactions 62, 1938, p. 19.)

[3] John Chrysostom Payne, born Jan. 1810, son of Capt John Payne and his wife Ismena, died a church student at Oscott, 11 Sept. 1824, aged fourteen. He was a model of edification, and was known as 'the St Aloysius of Oscott'. The portrait was an engraving showing him in cassock and surplice standing by a monumental tablet.

# 6

# THE PRIESTS OF HARVINGTON

Harvington must be one of the very few missions which has had priests continually in residence from the reign of James I down to the present day. It is also known that prior to 1603 the Pakingtons were occasionally served by visiting priests.[1]

JOHN FELTON aged seventy-four, was brought before the Protestant Bishop of Worcester, Whitgift, on 24 December 1582 and questioned about his activities. It seemed that he had the care of a Berkshire parish during Queen Mary's reign, but from 1561 had been in Leicestershire and Shropshire. At Nether Wallop in Hampshire he was under threat of being reported to the authorities and so travelled to Brian Fowler's house near Baswich on the outskirts of Stafford. Here at the farm standing on the site of the former St Thomas's Priory where 'divers lewd priests were resorting', he found David Pole, formerly Catholic Bishop of Peterborough, who reconciled Felton to the Church again. Thereafter Felton made Worcestershire his special care and stayed at various Catholic houses such as Upton Warren, Hindlip, Grafton and so on. He was known to Lady Throckmorton at Feckenham, Mrs Heath at Alvechurch and to Lady Windsor. At Christmas the previous year he had been with Mrs Pakington of Chaddesley.

> To all which places he resorted as occasion served ... After being examined how often he has said mass within this twelvemonth, he answered he cannot tell, but he sayeth, peradventure he hath sayed mass sundry times ... being asked who is the head of that Catholic Church he sayeth he cannot tell ... and being further examined by what authority he did reconcile the persons aforesaid he answereth, that he received authority by word from Doctor Allen beyond sea.[2]

We hear nothing more of John Felton who may well have died in prison. It is however just possible that Humphrey Pakington may have decided to move from his late father's house off the village street in Chaddesley to the more discreet surroundings of Harvington as the result of Felton's arrest.

SYMON SOUTHERN aged eighty-three or so was another priest who was also examined at Worcester along with John Felton. He was a stipendiary priest at Evesham who from 1559–1567 held the office of Steward of the Household at the Hospital of St Cross in Winchester. He had been a priest for fifty-one years but had not served any parish since the beginning of Elizabeth's reign. Since coming back to Worcestershire some eight years ago he had not been to church. He gave as an excuse his infirmities, but nevertheless admitted to having been with various people in Worcestershire where he had shriven and absolved 'divers after the old manner, when they had been sick'. Whether he visited the Pakingtons or not we cannot be certain. Other possible visitors were the Jesuits who had their headquarters nearby at Hindlip, the home of Humphrey Pakington's friend, Thomas Habington. They most probably included Fathers Garnet, Oldcorne, and Tesimond to be later implicated in the Gunpowder Plot, together with the laybrother Nicholas Owen.

[1] Veronica Webster, 'Two Marian Priests in Worcestershire' WR.1, April 1963, pp. 20–4; C. W. Clarke, 'Simon Southern at Hinton-on-the-Green' Worc. Recusant no. 16, Dec. 1970, pp. 2–6.

[2] William Allen (1532–94) Cardinal. He left England and concentrated on the work of training missionary priests for the conversion of their fellow countrymen from Protestantism, founding colleges at Douay and Rome for that purpose. He was created cardinal in 1587.

SAMUEL SMALLMAN c.1603–1613.[1] Smallman alias Emmanuel Johnson came from Shropshire, where in 1555 a John Smallman was bailiff of the manor of Ditton Priors belonging to the Pakingtons. In 1602 Samuel entered the English College in Rome and was ordained priest in August of the following year. The Chaddesley register records his burial on 15 May 1613 and notes that he 'was kylled falling of his horse on holy Thursday (i.e. Ascension Day, 13 May), being a Roman Catholik and a great traviler'. It is possible that Smallman was succeeded during the 1620s by a priest from Valladolid or Seville.

[1] Anstruther, G., *The Seminary Priests*, vol. 2, p. 173; Chaddesley Corbett Register.

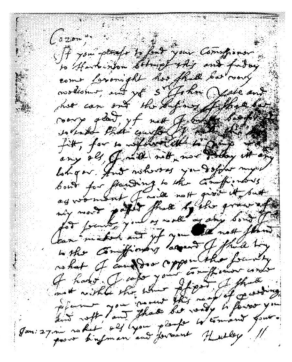

Humphrey Lutley's letter to Thomas Russell.

HUMPHREY LUTLEY *c.*1631. Humphrey was the son of John Lutley of Broncroft Castle, Shropshire, and Mary Pakington who married at Chaddesley on 17 June 1589. He was therefore Humphrey Pakington's nephew. During his chaplaincy at Harvington he acted ostensibly as steward or secretary and was permitted to travel into Holland together with the widowed Abigail Pakington (*c.*1580–1657) and her domestic servants. It is known that he was working again on the mission in Worcestershire or Staffordshire in 1643. He died at Harvington in 1653. The following is a letter written by him to Thomas Russell of Little Malvern Court. Thomas succeeded his father John in 1641. Its business-like tone suggests a man firmly in charge of affairs.

Cozen,
If you please to send your Commissioner to Harvington betwixt this and Friday come sevenight hee shall bee very welcome, and if Sir John Yate and hee can end the business I shall bee very glad. If nott, I must bee forward to take that course I will thinke fitt, for to referre itt to [*word illegible*] any els, I will nott.

And whereas you desire my bond for standing to the Commissioner's agreement, I will nott give itt, but my word passed shall by the grace of God serve you as well as any bond I can make. And if you will nott stand to the Commissioner's award, I shall try what I can doe upon the security I have. I[n] case your Commissioner come nott within the time prefixed, I shall presume you allow this way of proceeding, and rest, and shall bee ready to serve you what els you please to command your poore servant and kinsman H Lutley January 27.[1]

[1] Humphrey Lutley to Thomas Russell. St Helen's Record Office, Worcester, Berington 705:24/633/02. Humphrey's brother, Philip, was also a priest. He was ordained in Rome in 1624 and was Vicar General for Staffordshire and the neighbouring counties at the time of this death in 1684. Anstruther vol. 2, pp. 205–6; Hodgetts, 'The Yates of Harvington', *Recusant History* 22, p. 161, 1994–5.

MICHAEL JENNINGS 1632–1664.[1] Ordained in Rome, Jennings or Gennings, was sent to England in 1632, but he may have been the Michael Jennings who taught at Douay from 1646–1653. He was active in Worcestershire around the time of the Restoration, and John Kirk asserts that he came to Harvington.[2]

The following letter, which must date from around 1660, would seem to corroborate this:

Addressed: These for his honoured dear friend
Sir Charles Yate.
Honoured Sir: The holy man whose prayers I begged for you hath sent you his blessing in writing, which I have here enclosed. Judith Parker, Nan Parker's sister, who hath been deaf from her childhood, and dumb upon that account, hath recovered her hearing by his blessing and we are now teaching her to speak; also Jane Blofield is recovered from the torment of her tooth – ache which had tormented her many months. My Lady, Mrs. Yate, Mr. Audley and his sister were with the holy man in Cheshire. I beseech you present my most humble service to my Lady Yate, and give me the honour to be reckoned

Your humble servant
Michael Gennings[3]

Jennings probably died or moved from Harvington, as can be seen in the following entry.

Seventeenth-century rosary found under the floor of the Priest's room,
Harvington Hall.

[1] Gillow CRS vol. 17, p. 364. Anstruther, *The Seminary Priests*, vol. 2, p. 172.
[2] John Kirk, *Biographies of English Catholics in the 18th Century*, p. 95.
[3] M. Hodgetts, 'The Yates of Harvington', *Recusant History* 22, p. 169.

THOMAS CATTERALL ?1664. Catterall was ordained at Valladolid in 1644 and was sent to England in 1647. It is possible that he came to fill a vacancy at Harvington in 1664, since Anstruther quotes a Chapter minute of 29 August that year in which there is a resolution 'to write to Mr Manley that we shall lose my lady Yate's place and two or three dependent on her for want of one to send her, unless Mr Catterall be speedily procured to serve her.'[1] In her trust of 1677 it was arranged that the Dean and Chapter were to nominate and appoint priests to Harvington and Buckland.[2] Indeed procuring a suitable chaplain at this time was proving no easy task for Lady Yate. In writing to her son on 6th April (? 1668) she says that

I have heard since again from Mr. Waring (Dean of the Chapter 1660–1676) that's almost buries my hopes concerning Mr. Shepard, his coming into England being as yet uncertain, and advises taking hold of Mr. Fowler. I desire you inform me of his abilities, and chiefly his disposition, so far as you can, and how fit you conceive him for me. He shall not have cause at my house to bias as at Lyford, but if that be his humour to be partial [*deleted:*] that it is a great inconveniency in a house, I have experienced, and also quiet where it is not!'[3]

Whether Shepherd or Fowler ever came to Harvington is not known. Shepherd or Prance, as he was known, became a Chapterman and Vicar General of Warwickshire in 1672; Fowler, on the other hand, was in London in 1661 and died there in 1685.

It should perhaps be explained that after Elizabeth I had replaced the Catholic hierarchy with Protestant bishops English Catholics were without a bishop until the appointment in 1623 of William Bishop. As part of his restructuring programme this prelate erected a Dean and Chapter, which was subsequently confirmed by his successor, Bishop Richard Smith. After Smith's departure to France in the face of jurisdictional problems the exercise of episcopal and ordinary jurisdiction devolved upon the Dean and Chapter. In 1676 Dr John Perrott was elected Dean and in the following year, as mentioned above, signed an agreement with Lady Mary Yate regarding the appointment and support of the Harvington and Buckland priests (see Appendix III).

With Rome's appointment of John Leybourne as Vicar Apostolic (i.e. holding delegated rather than ordinary episcopal powers) in 1685 the Chapter ceased to have any effective power and its position became purely honorary. It continues to exist today on a philanthropic basis as The Old Brotherhood of the Secular Clergy.

[1] Anstruther, vol. 2, p. 49.
[2] See Appendix III.
[3] Hodgetts, 'The Yates of Harvington', *Recusant History* 22, pp. 168-9.

ST JOHN WALL *c.*1671-1678.[1] John Wall has been venerated as 'The Martyr of Harvington' since the nineteenth century – a devotion that has grown since the canonisation of the Forty Martyrs in 1970. The Saint's link with the Hall, however, is not documented, although as it will be seen, he was clearly working in the neighbourhood. John was born in 1620, the son of William Wall, a Catholic landowner in Norfolk, and Dorothy, his wife. The family, it appears, had moved to Lancashire to find a more congenial religious climate, and it was here that John was baptised by the Jesuit, Edmund Arrowsmith, who a few years later was martyred at Lancaster. Aged thirteen John was sent to

St John Wall by Gabrielle Mewburn Mercer, 2004.

Douay and from there he went on to study philosophy and theology at the English College in Rome. A short while after he was followed by his brother William, who also became a student for the secular priesthood, but transferred to the Benedictines, eventually dying at the Abbey of Lamspring in Hanover in 1704.

Meanwhile John was ordained priest on December 1645, and after further studies left for England three years later. In the course of his journey he passed through Douay and visited the Franciscan friary there with the intention of joining the Friars Minor. It was not until the following year that he was able to return, and on 1 January, 1651, he received the habit as a novice, taking the name of Br Joachim of St Anne.

In due course Wall made his profession and was given the offices of Father Vicar and Novice and Junior Master in the community. A small group of friars led by Leo Randolph and Joachim of St Anne (who now called himself Webb or Johnson for reasons of security) crossed over to England in 1656. They headed for Randolph's home at Wood Bevington in Warwickshire, and from there dispersed to Yorkshire, Worcestershire, Warwickshire and Staffordshire. Wall was assigned to Worcestershire, but extended his work to Staffordshire and Gloucestershire, preferring to be an itinerant missionary rather than live as a permanent chaplain in gentry houses. He nevertheless visited Coughton, and Father John Brownlow of Harvington writing up his memoirs in 1874, places the martyr among 'Priests of Harvington and the neighbourhood'. The dates 1671–1678 then represent the years in which Wall would most likely have visited Harvington, possibly staying briefly at the Hall. Yet a later chaplain, Dr Charles Dodd, himself an eminent historian, writing a mere forty years after Wall's death, makes no mention of such a link with the Hall.[2] Instead, the following facts may well lead us to think that Father Brownlow was recording an oral tradition, as indeed he did on other historical matters. A Franciscan breviary was found in a farmhouse in Harvington about 1890 and given to Canon Wheatley at Kidderminster who gave it to the Harvington priest, Father C Harris.

The breviary had come into the canon's possession about 1890, brought to him by one of his parishioners, a poor Irishwoman who worked for some small farmer or market gardener at Harvington. It had been among their family books for a very long time and no one knew how it came to be there. The farmer's wife gave it to the Irish woman. The initials FPI on the cover and the date 1651 point to the martyr's ownership. The initials would stand for 'Frater Pater

St John Wall's breviary.

Joachim'; since Franciscan priests were called 'Brother' (Frater) in addition to 'Father' (Pater) and 'J' is often written as 'I' in Latin. The date, too, could refer to the date on which Wall was admitted as a novice, that is, 1 January 1651. Rather more substantial evidence of his association with the Harvington area is provided by the circumstances of his arrest, which happened at Rushock Court, a mere two and a half miles from Harvington and within the boundaries of our present day parish. The embroidered chasuble said to have belonged to St John Wall and now belonging to the parish, was only presented to St Mary's in the 1940s and came from the Coughton area. It could date from the late seventeenth century and it does have the Franciscan motif (the arms of Christ and St Francis) on the back.[3]

In August 1678 Charles II was warned of a 'popish plot' against his own Protestant subjects' lives. Details of this alleged plot were readily provided by a scoundrel named Titus Oates. At the same time the mysterious death of a Protestant magistrate Sir Edmund Berry Godfrey, helped to fuel the popular imagination and led to the imprisonment and execution of innocent Catholics.

John Wall was in London for a Franciscan provincial chapter when, in the last week of October, a proclamation was issued requiring all Catholics to leave the capital by the end of the following week. Wall accordingly made for Worcestershire and the house of a Mr Finch, who was the tenant of Rushock Court. The farmhouse behind the church now stands on part of the site and possibly incorporates some of the vanished and extensive manor house. Both farm and church are visible from Harvington. It was here that on the night of 9 December the house was raided by the sheriff's deputy and seven or eight men in search of 'a gentleman of that house for his debts'. The priest, who was still in bed, was arrested by mistake, but was then recognised by a soldier who said he had been a servant there seven years before. This detail points to the fact that Wall was no stranger to Rushock and to the countryside around Harvington. From Rushock the sheriff and his men proceeded to take Wall before the magistrate called Townsend at the neighbouring village of Elmley Lovett. Two Justices were needed for the committal to prison and so ironically it was Sir John Pakington, a Protestant cousin of Lady Yate, who lived at Westwood Park, near Droitwich who resolved the matter. The priest refused to take the proffered oaths of allegiance and supremacy and was imprisoned in Worcester Castle. Brought before the assizes in the following April, Wall was charged with refusing the oaths and as a suspected priest. Three reluctant witnesses and one other, 'of his own accord for lucre's sake', testified against him, so that the jury found him guilty of exercising his priesthood.

He was condemned to be hanged, drawn and quartered, but first had to go to London to be questioned by Oates and his accomplice, Bedloe, who failed to implicate him in any way in their so-called plot. Back in Worcester the martyr was informed that he was to die on 22 August, which news 'he embraced with a joyful heart, for that it happened on a Friday (a day on which Our Lord suffered), and likewise the Octave Day of the Glorious Virgin's Assumption, to whom he had been all his life singularly devoted'. So on that August day in 1679 St John set out on his last earthly journey to the gallows on Red Hill overlooking the city.[4] His butchered body was buried in St Oswald's churchyard, just outside the city Foregate, where it was noticed that for sometime afterwards the grass grew green over his grave while the rest of the churchyard was bare. The grave is now probably under the northern footpath of the road, but a memorial tablet on a wall nearby recalls the burial. A small relic of the saint has been placed in the altarstone of St Mary's, Harvington. At the beginning of the Second World War, a memorial crucifix was erected in the garden of 4 Whittington Road, on the site of the gibbet where St John and other Worcestershire martyrs died. This was due to the efforts of Mrs Ellen Grant Ferris, who was also responsible for the plaque on St Oswald's cemetery in the Tything. Devotions were held by the memorial site for some time in the 1950s.

[1]   Bishop Challoner, *Memoirs of Missionary Priests*, (new edn), Pollen, pp. 550–5, 565. 1924; Camm, *Forgotten Shrines*, pp. 262–5, 268–74.
[2]   Dodd, *Church History*, vol. 3, p. 311; Gillow CRS vol. 17, pp. 364–5.
[3]   Cf. 'Note on Embroidery from Harvington 18th- (sic) century chasuble from Sambourne' by HR Hodgkinson FSN, Oxford, 1946. The chasuble is now on exhibition in the Hall. Birmingham Archaeological Society Transactions 44 (1941–2), pp. 121–2
[4]   Cf. speech from the scaffold, Appendix IV.

SYLVESTER JENKS 1686–1687.[1] The future bishop-elect of Callipolis *in partibus* was born in Shropshire *c*.1656. At an early age Jenks was sent to Douay, where on 15 August 1675 he took the missionary oath under the name of Medcalfe. At some point he came to the notice

Sylvester Jenks, 1692.

of Lady Mary Yate at Harvington who undertook to make a substantial contribution to meet the expenses of his education.[2] The young man made rapid progress and on the completion of his studies was appointed professor of philosophy. His ordination to the priesthood took place on 23 September 1684. After teaching for six years, Jenks was sent to England and to the mission at Harvington. It must have been something of a disappointment to Lady Yate that Sylvester Jenks's chaplaincy lasted no more than a year, for as a result of a sermon preached in Worcester before James II on 24 August 1687 he was summoned to London and appointed one of the king's preachers in ordinary with a salary from the Exchequer of £60 a year. Three of his sermons preached before the king at Whitehall and Windsor survive; they deal with the Eucharist and Transubstantiation. The revolution of 1688 however necessitated his leaving for Flanders where he lived until times became quieter.

On his return he lived in or near London and was appointed chapter archdeacon of Surrey and Kent. In London he seems to have been chiefly occupied with matters of private controversy, particularly regarding the Jansenist heresy, but he also wrote a number of works on morality and a treatise on the Catechism of the Council of Trent. His abilities and strict religious life so impressed his brethren that in 1711 he was proposed by Bishops Giffard and Witham for the vicariate of the Northern District. On 13 August, Propaganda unanimously elected Jenks to fill this vacancy and papal consent was given on 22 August 1713. Unfortunately, Jenks became seriously ill and his consecration was deferred. He died in December of the following year, aged fifty-eight.

The Harvington historian, Dodd, remarks that Sylvester Jenks was remarkable for the clearness of his conceptions, his well-balanced mind and elegance of language. His theological learning and abilities were eminent and his religious life was an example of solid piety and sterling humanity. In the preface to his book on 'Blind Obedience' Jenks wrote:

I keep my name to myself, and my reason is, because I love a quiet life. I ever looked upon it as the greatest blessing which a bad world can afford, and am persuaded that being private is the easiest and securest way of being quiet. Besides, I see no good there is in being talked of, either well or ill. The one is good for nothing but to make a man vain; the other is apt to make him vexed; all to no purpose.[3]

¹ Gillow, *Biographical Dictionary* vol. 3, pp. 616–21; Anstruther, vol. 3, pp. 114–17.

² Cf. indenture dated 10 February 1686 between Dame Mary Yate and Silvester Jenks providing him with an annuity of £45, but this must refer to post ordination studies, Appendix III.

³ *God's safe way of obedience*, revised and edited by a priest. London, Thomas Richardson, 1872.

WILLIAM HARRIS *c.*1692–1697.¹ Harris, also known as Daniel, was sent to England in 1685. A Chapter list of 1692 mentions the 'Mr Daniel of Douay dwelleth with my Lady Yate constantly.' It is to him that we owe an inventory of the chapel furnishings made after Lady Yates's death in 1696, and in October of the following year he added the first reference to Harvington library:

All the books left at Harvington markt M:Lady Yate are likewise for the use of the clergy man that shall assist as above. So answered Madame Apollonia Yate, Executrix to ye Lady Yate, being askt by me William Daniel in October 1697.

¹ Anstruther, vol. 3, p. 153; CRS 9, p. 113; BAAc.155 (*Recusant History* 22, pp. 174–51).

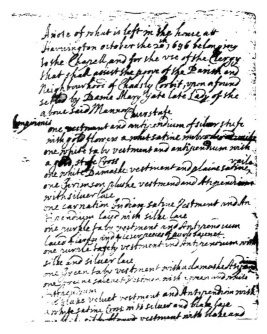

William Harris's chapel inventory, 1696.

JOHN MORGAN *c*.1703.[1] Morgan is probably to be identified with a priest named Morgan Johnson who was living in Worcestershire in 1699 and 1701. It is also likely that he had been chaplain to Lord Aston at Tixall. A note dated 26 August 1703 and signed 'John Morgan' records that he had delivered to Apollonia Yate 'two lockets of Diamonds ... to be kept by her and restor'd for the use they were Design'd for.' On 20 March 1706/7 Apollonia entrusted the lockets to her niece Mary, Lady Throckmorton, who signed a receipt stating that they were 'left in the custody of my said Aunt by my deare Grandmother Yate for the use of the Parish Church of Chaddesley Corbitt when Catholicke' (i.e. in expectation of a return to Catholicism). Possibly the lockets were in fact reliquaries. Of Morgan it was said that 'he was learned and well able to give advice to his brethren'.[2] John Morgan was buried at Chaddesley Corbett on 29 January 1718.

[1] Hodgetts, M., *Recusant History* 22, 1994–5, p. 171.
[2] Kirk, p. 169.

ROBERT HEYDON 1712–1714.[1] Heydon was born in Gloucestershire on 13 January 1683 and was the son of Francis and Christian Heydon. He entered Douay on 26 October 1697, assuming the alias of Collington. Sent as a deacon to St Gregory's, Paris, he was ordained priest there at Whitsun 1708.

After graduation he left for England and Harvington in October 1712. An inventory of chapel furnishings of 14 February 1714 refers to him: 'An account of what C. Plate I received from Mr Heydon, Mr Morgan present': and ending 'This is a true Account of what I deliver'd to Mr Bennet, Witness my hand, Robert Heydon.' The other reference is in connection with the Harvington Library.

> All the books in ye Upper Library (except some few Italian books, which belong to Sir Robert (Throckmorton) and a parcel of old books of Mr Robert Heydon's and what are in a glass case in ye P(riest's?) room belong to the said solicitor Sec. Cler. and his successors. Tho' many books have ye Kinns' name in them, yet they were given by Kinn (I believe) to ye said library, or purchased of Mr Heydon's sisters by ... Desunt Reliqua.[2]

Heydon left Harvington in 1714, returning to St Gregory's, obtaining a doctorate in 1718. He died in London on 13 October 1718, having just returned from Paris, and was buried at St Pancras on 15 October.

[1] BAA c260.
[2] Kirk, p. 119.

WILLIAM THOMSON 1714–1726.[1] William was a Norfolk man, the son of William and Frances Thomson, and was born *c*.1667. In the will of Edward Preston he is called 'William Thompson of Lyme Regis', which may well have been his home town. He made his profession of faith at Douay on 14 September 1709, assuming the aliases of Temple and Bennett. Ordained priest, he is said to have left for England in 1712, but an investigation into Jansenism at the college in November that year shows that he was still there. The visitators left on All Souls Day (2 November) and 'were extremely pleased with Mr Temple and talked some several times afterwards about, saying that he'd make a most excellent missioner, he has such an honest way with him'. It is clear from the inventory mentioned above that Thomson alias Bennett was at Harvington in 1714. He died here on 28 September 1726 and was succeeded by Dodd, who had been assisting him since 1722.

[1] Gillow CRS vol. 17, p. 366. Anstruther, vol. 3, p. 224.

HUGH TOOTELL (CHARLES DODD) 1722–1743.[1] Tootell, who is better known by his alias Charles Dodd, came from a Lancashire family and was born in 1671. He was the nephew of a much revered missioner, Christopher Tootell, who laboured for some thirty years at Ladywell, the ancient and celebrated shrine of Our Lady at Fernyhalgh, not far from Preston. Dodd went to the college at Douay in 1688, and from there proceeded to follow the usual course of philosophy and theology at St Gregory's Seminary, Paris. He obtained his BD at the Sorbonne, and during the vacation preparatory to the licence for the DD he returned to Douay, on 6 June 1697. After his ordination to the priesthood he left for the English mission, working for a time with his uncle at Fernyhalgh and then as chaplain at Mossborough Hall, Lancashire. As mentioned above, he moved to Harvington in 1722 to help William Thomson, who by that time was in ailing health. Dodd spent much of his time at Harvington in writing. Here, in the course of thirty years, he arranged the materials for and finished his celebrated *The Church History of England 1500–1688*.

This was originally in three folio volumes, and was newly edited in 1839–43 by Canon Mark Tierney. The *History* was attacked by a Jesuit as being unfair to the Society, but they had already been nettled some years earlier by Dodd's short *History of the English College at Douay* (London, 1713), written as if by the Protestant chaplain of an English regiment at the siege and capture of that town. This had been followed in 1715 by an even more provocative work entitled *The Secret Policy of the Jesuits*. *The Secret Policy* was discovered in a series of attempts against the secular clergy; it is in eight parts and twenty-four letters directed to the Jesuit Provincial, each part containing three letters. *The Secret Policy* is in fact often called *Dodd's Provincial Letters* and of course evoked a riposte, which, however, was never printed. Dodd's antipathy earned for himself the epithets of 'groundless forger, notorious falsifier, base spreader of calumnies'. The nineteenth-century antiquarian Dr George Oliver, in particular, stigmatised *The Secret Policy* as 'a scurrilous libel' and added: 'It is certain that Mr Dodd is a dishonest historian, very deficient in Christian charity, and a stranger to the feelings and language of a gentleman.' It should, perhaps, be said that Dr Oliver was a priest with strong Jesuit sympathies, who had in fact spent some time teaching at Stonyhurst College. A more impartial and charitable view was given by the prominent Catholic layman, Charles Butler, who explained that Dodd wrote at a time when the secular clergy were suffering under charges of Jansenism, which they supposed were inspired by the Jesuits, in order to install themselves at Douay, as they had done in 1578 in the college founded for the secular clergy in Rome.[2] A total of sixty-five works are listed by Gillow, but others exist in mss; they include, in addition to those mentioned above, a number of doctrinal and catechetical writings, as well as material for biographies of English Catholics. The small room in the Hall at Harvington, lit by a large Georgian window and lined on one side with bookshelves has become known as 'Dr Dodd's Library'; the tradition is that he worked there, and no doubt some of his books were stored there. It also contains one of the more ingenious hides of the Hall formerly concealed in a large cupboard. This was only discovered in 1894 by Bernard Lloyd, grandson of Edward Hailes senior, who was living with his grandfather, tenant of the Hall Farm c.1870–1897. Anstruther quotes an undated letter from Dodd to the agent in Rome which he assigns to 1742 to show that Dodd was not at that time residing at the Hall. The letter mentions a youth at the English College in Rome whose father's name was Parker and a farmer 'in whose house

THE

# CHURCH HISTORY

OF

# *E N G L A N D,*

From the Year 1500, to the Year 1688.

Chiefly with regard to

# C A T H O L I C K S:

BEING

A Complete ACCOUNT of the Divorce, Supremacy, Diffolution of Monafteries, and firft Attempts for a Reformation under King *Henry* VIII. the unfettled State of the Reformation under *Edward* VI. the Interruption it met with from Queen *Mary*; with the laft Hand put to it by Queen *Elifabeth*:

TOGETHER WITH

The various Fortunes of the CATHOLICK CAUSE, During the REIGNS of

King *James* I. King *Charles* I. King *Charles* II. and King *James* II.

PARTICULARLY,

The LIVES of the moft eminent Catholicks, Cardinals, Bifhops, Inferior Clergy, Regulars, and Laymen, who have diftinguifhed themfelves by their Piety, Learning, or Military Abilities:

ALSO,

A Diftinct and Critical ACCOUNT of the Works of the LEARNED: The TRIALS of thofe that fuffered either on the Score of Religion, or for Real or Fictitious Plots againft the Government:

WITH

The FOUNDATION of all the *Englifh* Colleges and Monafteries abroad.

The Whole fupported by Original PAPERS and LETTERS; many whereof were never before made Publick.

To which is Prefixed,

A GENERAL HISTORY of Ecclefiaftical Affairs under the *Britifh*, *Saxon*, and *Norman* Periods.

In EIGHT PARTS.

The FIRST VOLUME.

*B R U S S E L S:*

Printed in the Year MDCCXXXVII.

Title page of Dodd's *Church History* 1737–1742.

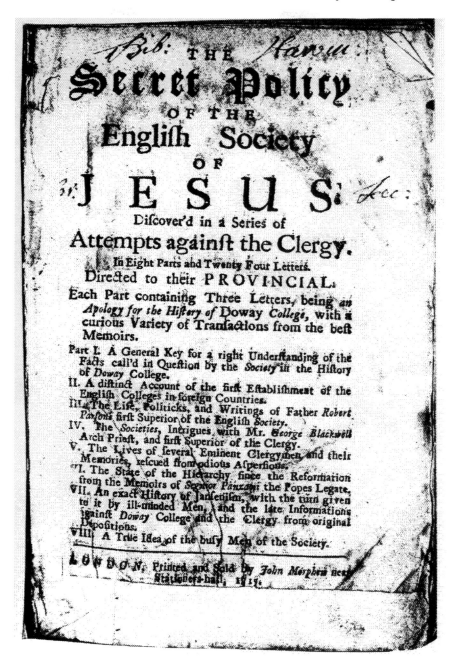

Title page of Dodd's *Secret Policy* 1715.

I reside'. However, Dodd, worn out with the troubles his work brought upon him, died at Harvington on 27 February, 1742/3, aged sixty-one. The Chaddesley register records his burial on March 1742.

¹ Gillow, *Biographical Dictionary*, vol. 5, pp. 549–555; Berington, J., *The Memoirs of Gregorio Panzani*, Birmingham, 1793, pp viii–xii.
² In 1686 The Rev Christopher Tootell, James Dimmock and Andrew Giffard went to reside at a newly acquired chapel in Lime Street, London. Defamed by the Jesuits as holding unorthodox opinions, all three priests were forced out after only six months. Dodd would have been aware of his uncle's ill treatment at the hands of the Society. Gillow, *Biographical Dictionary* vol. 2, pp. 451–2.

THOMAS   ATHERTON   1739–1743.¹   Atherton   came   from Lancashire, having been born in 1706. He studied at Douay and was ordained priest in 1732. He was then sent on the mission, where he worked in the Midland District, spending four years at Harvington as assistant to Dodd. After the latter's death he moved to Wolverhampton, where he died in 1758.

¹ Anstruther, vol. 4, p. 14.

CHARLES FITZWILLIAM 1743–1750 (known later as Williams).¹ Atherton's successor, who was born in Middlesex in 1700, was a student at the English College, Rome, where he was ordained in 1729. He died in 1750 and apparently at Harvington, but there is no record of this in the Chaddesley register.

In a letter, Bishop Stonor asserted roundly that the power of the nomination at Harvington resided in the Bishop and not the owner, Sir Robert Throckmorton. This was correct, as the jurisdiction of the Old Chapter in such matters now belonged to the Vicars Apostolic. When Stonor dismissed Mr Williams from Wolverhampton on the account of 'his haughty, passionate and quarrelsome behaviour which was such that there was no living under the same roof with him' he sent him to live 'sort of hermit' at Harvington and merely wrote to Sir Robert 'very civilly remarking that I should send somebody to Harvington that would be disagreeable to him but intimating sufficiently at the same time that the nomination in no way belonged to him'. Mr Williams found repeated excuses for delay but eventually obeyed. ²

¹ Gillow, CRS vol. 17, p. 367.
² Marie Rowlands, 'The Staffordshire Clergy 1688–1803', *Recusant History* 9 no. 5, April, 1968, Ref BAA-C470.

JAMES LAYFIELD 1750–1751.[1] A Lancashire man, he was born in 1707. After studying classics in England he was accepted at the English College at the request of Cardinal Gualtieri. Pope Benedict XIII ordained him to the priesthood on 16 March 1726. Two years later Layfield became confessor to the nuns at Liege, but eventually left for the English Mission. At first he was stationed at Wolverhampton, but helped briefly at Harvington. In 1752 he was chosen canon, settling at Oscott where he died on 5 February 1756. He was a member of the Chapter and much esteemed by all that knew him.

[1] Kirk, p. 149.

GEORGE BISHOP 1750–1752.[1] He belonged to the Bishop family of Brailes and studied at Douay and St Gregory's, Paris, where he took the seminary oath in 1717. Coming on the mission, he first lived at Brailes and after that at Irnham, in 1742–4. On the death of Charles Fitzwilliam he succeeded him at Harvington but was back again at Brailes soon after. He died at Marnhull, Dorset, on 16 August 1768. George Bishop was Vicar General to Bishop Stonor in Oxfordshire, and as a member of the Chapter was archdeacon of Hereford and Shropshire. He wrote a work on *Moral Philosophy* and translated Lambert's *Maniere d'instruire les pauvres de la Campagne,* neither of which was apparently published, though both were considered to have great merit. Bishop did publish Father Anselm Mannock's, *Poor Man's Catechism* (1752) and very likely *The Poor Man's Controversy.*

[1] Gillow, *Biographical Dictionary*, vol. 1, p. 218; Kirk, p. 26.

The following was a local priest but never on the Harvington Mission.

FRANCIS PARKER 1740–1779.[1] Born *c.*1740 at Bluntington, near Harvington, where a family of that name lived till the end of the eighteenth century. He studied at Douay and then Paris, where he took his licentiate in Divinity. He then became chaplain to Lord Arundell at Irnham, Lincolnshire, 'where he was much esteemed both by that noble family and by a numerous congregation'. In the latter part of his short life, a stroke left him paralysed down one side but he survived for six or seven years, incapable of performing any pastoral duty. He then retired to his friends in Worcestershire and died there in September 1779, being buried in Chaddesley on 5 September: 'Mr Francis Parker, Romish Priest' (Chaddesley Register).

[1] Kirk, p. 176.

ARTHUR VAUGHAN 1752–1792.[1] Vaughan, the longest-serving priest at Harvington in the eighteenth century, was born in London on 14 February 1724. Educated at Douay, he was ordained priest in 1749, and returned to England to teach for a while at Bishop Challoner's School at Standon Lordship. He was then appointed to succeed George Bishop at Harvington in 1752. Sometime in the 1750s he founded a school for girls at the Hall, which he placed under the management of a Miss Ainsworth. A few years later the school moved to what is now Maryvale House, four miles north of Birmingham.

Interestingly, Vaughan and the Harvington mission are mentioned twice in the diary of a French diplomat, the Marquis de Bombelles, who came here in August 1784. The marquis's impressions of Mass in the Georgian chapel have already been referred to, but the diary goes on to describe Vaughan in unflattering terms as 'short and fat', and the priest's rooms as unsuitable for a man of his station. Whether the diarist was referring to the North Tower, or the rooms on the top floor of the Hall used by Vaughan's predecessors of two hundred years before is not clear.

It is to Vaughan that we owe the oldest surviving register. Commencing in 1752, this Register is supplemented by lists of Easter Communicants written into it which helps to give some idea of our Mass-goers in the eighteenth century.[2]

Interestingly, it shows that there was already a substantial Irish element in 1752, drawn from Kidderminster and Stourbridge, both of which towns were then served by Harvington. Marriages are not included until 1804, when the chapel was licensed for them. Before that time and up until 1837 they had to take place in the Anglican parish church, although it was usual to anticipate this ceremony with a service before a Catholic priest. Confirmations by various vicars apostolic are carefully recorded.

Some slight pieces of literature were produced by Arthur Vaughan; the first was a poem in '8 books' called *The Triumph of the Cross,* which was inspired by the story of St Mary of Egypt. The departure of a Jesuit, Fr Charles Wharton, from the Catholic chapel at Sansom Fields in Worcester, and his abandonment of the priesthood, occasioned *The Ghost of Sansom Fields*; and finally, Martin Madan's treatise advocating polygamy published in 1780 stirred Vaughan to a lighthearted response entitled *Madan's The Thelypthora burlesqued.* Arthur Vaughan died at Harvington on 17 July 1792 aged sixty-eight and was buried in St Cassian's, Chaddesley on 28 July.

After Vaughan's death Bishop Talbot asked the learned John Kirk to go to Harvington. Gillow remarks that 'this appointment was eminently suitable to his (Kirk's) tastes, for it was the glory of Harvington to have been served by an unbroken line of literary chaplains from the reign of James II, and above all, it was here that Hugh Tootell, alias Dodd, wrote his *Church History,* the confirmation of which was the absorbing interest of Mr. Kirk's life'. However, while Kirk was awaiting improvements to his accommodation in the Hall he was called upon to become president of the school at Sedgley Park where he had once been a pupil and later, chaplain. Kirk eventually became Bishop Berington's secretary and pastor of the new mission at Lichfield. He is remembered chiefly for his *Biographies of English Catholics in the Eighteenth Century,* a continuation of his mentor, Dodd. For this and other labours Gregory XVI made him a doctor of divinity. Kirk died in 1851 at the age of ninety-two, having lived to see the restoration of the Hierarchy.

[1] Kirk, p. 241. Gillow, *Biographical Dictonary*, vol. 5, p. 564.
[2] CRS vol. 17, pp. 370–422.

RICHARD CORNTHWAITE 1792–1803.[1] Cornthwaite, a Lancastrian, born in 1736, studied at Douay where he was ordained priest in 1765. For a short time he taught at Sedgley Park, but went on to succeed Bishop Thomas Talbot at Brockington near Havant. He was later appointed procurator at St Omer's (1782–1792), where his service to the college was much valued. In the early days of the French Revolution attempts were made by the Jacobins to involve him in plots against the Convention; a letter with Cornthwaite's forged signature was apparently dropped on the ramparts, where it was discovered and produced as evidence of treason. At that point Cornthwaite prudently decided to return to England, settling at Harvington, where he died on 11 September 1803. The Chaddesley register gives his burial date as 28 September.

He described himself in a letter of 9 June 1792 as 'of a corpulent habit and often indisposed, stands in need of much bodily exercise, is fond of shooting, fishing etc under the pretence of preserving his health.' He was the first priest to enjoy the improvements carried out by Sir John Throckmorton at the instigation of Kirk who was to have gone to Harvington.

[1] Kirk, pp. 58–9.

GEORGE HARTLEY 1803–1806.[1] Richard and Elizabeth Hartley had
two sons who entered the priesthood: Thomas and William. A
nephew, George, 'young, strong and rosy' (Brownlow), likewise
became a priest, studied first at Sedgley Park and went on to Lisbon
were he was ordained. On his return to England, Hartley was
appointed chaplain to Robert Berkeley at Spetchley.[2] He moved to
Harvington in 1803, where he died on 26 June 1806 (28 June Brownlow) aged thirty-six. 'The Revd Geo. Hartley, Catholic Priest' was
buried in Chaddesley on 30 June.[3]

[1] Gillow CRS vol. 17, p. 369.
[2] Spetchley Park near Worcester, was a Catholic chaplaincy from the late seventeenth century It was mostly served by Jesuits until the nineteenth century. It
remains a Mass centre.
[3] The Chaddesley Register gives the incorrect date 31 June.

JOHN CORNE 1806–1816.[1] John and his brother James came from
Betley in Staffordshire. Both studied at Douay, John being ordained
in 1776. James became spiritual director at Sedgley Park, and in
1783 was appointed to Shrewsbury, while John lived at Cobridge in
the Potteries, where he built a chapel. In 1784 he moved to Stafford
and also built a chapel there. John Corne was one of fifteen Staffordshire priests who became known as the 'Staffordshire Clergy'.[2] They
were sympathetic to a lay-led 'Catholic Committee' whose aim was
to restrict the powers of Rome in the interest of securing toleration
for English Catholics. The Committee, it was also asserted, was
attempting to give the laity equal authority to their pastors in matters
pertaining to every part of church discipline. In this movement Harvington's lord of the manor, Sir John Throckmorton, was a prominent protagonist, writing a series of pamphlets in the Committee's
defence, and promptly opposed with another series by the Midland
District's Vicar Apostolic, John Milner. Milner was, in fact, reluctant to accept his appointment to the District in 1803, but eventually
these (in Milner's eyes) schismatic tendencies died away, along with
the membership of the 'Staffordshire Clergy'. It is nevertheless interesting to note that, after leaving Stafford and a brief stay in Linley,
John Corne came to Harvington in 1806, while another former priest
of the group, Joseph Berington, ended his days as chaplain at Buckland. Corne himself died on 4 August 1816, aged sixty-eight. He
was buried in St Cassian's in Chaddesley Corbett three days later.
James died four months later. Of James, Bishop Milner said that 'he
was all soul, John all body. James was desirous of solid knowledge,

John of gossip'.

The following letter from Bishop Milner and dated 23 June 1810, was addressed to Corne at Harvington Hall

Dr Sir,

I am sorry to learn, by a second letter from you on the subject, the inadequacy of your income to your wants, as likewise your unwillingness to accept of the only vacant place I know of in the District, namely Mr Turville's at Husbands Bosworth.[3] The fact is that many others of our clergy are in the same predicament, and more or less all the Bishops. We all experience that necessaries of life and the taxes encrease, while our income instead of encreasing is constantly diminished. You will conclude that this must be the case with respect to the Bishops when I inform you that there is not one of us who lives in the style you do. Bishop Gibson keeps a man but no horse. I keep a horse but no man, and the other Bishops keep neither man nor horse, whilst you keep both. I do not say this Dr Sir, by way of reproach, as I wish yr comforts to be encreased and not diminished, but by way of shewing the hardships of the times. – I recollect desiring you to get the books belonging to the clergy of this District at Harvington put in order, by way of indemnifying you and at the same time of contributing to your immediate relief I send you the enclosed draft for 10£. –I have at the same time to inform you that Mr Potts, of his own accord, and without any communication with me, applied some time ago to Sir John Throckmorton for his consent to remove the said Books from Harvington to Oscott, for his own use and that of the other master of the latter place, and that Sir John returned him for an answer that he had no objection to the proposal. I, on my part, have said the same.

Hence you may expect that Mr Walsh will, one of these days send a cart over to Harvington to take away the said Books: but, in the mean time Messrs Potts and Walsh beg you will take the first opportunity of sending them the Catalogue of the Library which they beg you will direct to the former to the care of Mr Wilks Bookseller New Street Birmingham

The said Gentn. both desire their Comp.ts to you. I remain, Dr Sir, Your most faithfully humble Ser.t
J Milner

P.S. Nerquiss is given up, Mr Price is appointed to Swinnerton – Moseley is supplied.[4]

Rev Mr Corne
Harvington Hall
near Kidderminster
Worcestershire

[1]  Kirk, p. 58; Gillow CRS vol. 8, p. 342.
[2]  M. Rowlands, 'The Staffordshire Clergy 1688–1803', *Recusant History* 9 no. 5, April 1968. Also, Gooch, Leo (ed.), *The Revival of English Catholicism*: The Staffordshire Faction or Appellants Lettsr 19. Bannister to Rutter, Mowbreck 2 July 1798, after hearing of Bishop Berington's death.
[3]  The ancient Catholic family of the Turvilles of Leicestershire acquired Husband's Bosworth in 1763.
[4]  Nerquiss was a Giffard property in Flintshire, while Swynnerton and Moseley in Staffordshire were other country-house chaplaincies. BAAC 1849.

JOHN MARSDEN 1816–1824.[1] Marsden was born in Derbyshire in 1790. His parents were both Protestants and John Marsden became a Catholic while still a boy. Educated at Sedgley Park and Oscott, he was ordained priest in 1817. On the death of the Rev John Corne he was assigned to the Harvington mission, where he acted as chaplain to Sir John Throckmorton. The writer of his obituary informs us that at Harvington:

he found a field open for his assiduity, and like a true minister of Christ, he determined to avail himself of the opportunity that presented itself to him. He found his congregation, (particularly the lower classes) plunged either in ignorance, or, if the expression may be allowed, in a kind of supine negligence: the Catholic children were either forced to attend Protestant schools, and go to church, or be deprived of education. This was an evil he resolved if possible to remedy ... From this period up to his last illness, his labours with regard to his flock have been indefatigable. But his grand aim was for the erection of a new chapel, the old one proving too small for the accommodation of his numerous converts, and the great increase of the Irish population of Kidderminster. His strenuous exertions in the erection of this chapel, which is now in a state of great forwardness, tended no doubt considerably to impair a constitution naturally weak; but which yet had appeared as an impregnable rock against the gates of heresy. He bore his last illness with great courage, patience, and resignation becoming a true minister.[2]

His successor, John Brownlow, recorded in his diary:

1824, March 22nd; the Revd John Marsden, pastor of Harvington, my respected friend, died. He was interred in the New Chapel there, which was being erected. The walls were up, and the roof on; but the plastering was not done, nor the floor laid. I then, for some months had the care of his people; visiting them from Stourbridge.

It was in the year previous to Marsden's death that the disastrous fire destroyed part of the Georgian Chapel and its precious contents.

Surprisingly, no memorial to this pioneer priest, whose life was cut short at the age of thirty-four, was erected in St Mary's; or if there was such a stone or plaque let into the floor, it is not visible today. It is likely that he lies buried before the altar as was often the custom.

[1] Gillow, CRS vol. 17, p. 369.
[2] *The Catholic Miscellany*, vol. 13, p. 254.

JOHN THOMAS BROWNLOW 1824–1875. Brownlow holds a special place in the history of Harvington, largely because of his prolific writings, including a little book of 'Memoranda culled from various sources', and, of course, his long tenure of the mission.[1] In his notes Brownlow tells us that he was born on Maundy Thursday, 2 April 1795, at Harby in Lincolnshire, the son of Thomas and Mary Brownlow. He was baptised the next day, that is Good Friday.

A natural scholar, Brownlow would have gone to Cambridge and probably taken Holy Orders in the Anglican Church had not he come in contact with a French émigré priest.

The young man's frequent discussions with the priest and much studying of works of controversy led to his embracing the Catholic faith and the abandonment of all thought of university. In 1816 he entered Oscott and four years later was ordained priest by Bishop Milner for whom he always retained a strong affection.

John Brownlow was first assigned to the new mission at Stourbridge, where a small garret was acquired for the celebration of Mass. At first, he used to walk fifteen miles every Saturday from his lodgings in Bloxwich in order to be there for the people on Sunday. He would walk back to Bloxwich on the following day. He records that on 2 September 1820, the Stourbridge mission was formally separated from the ancient centre at Harvington.

Rev John Brownlow.

With Milner's permission the intrepid missioner set out to find benefactors for the new chapel. Not content with visiting the surrounding towns and villages, he left on a cold January day in 1822 to make 'my great Northern Excursion', which took him as far as Newcastle-on-Tyne.

I rode on my swift, sprightly, gay, beautiful, frolicksome, brown Welsh pony! who soon became an entertaining beggar; flying up to the mansion in the highest style of fashion, and with all the liveliest and most winning gesticulations and expressions of profound respect; telling the admiring Squire how delighted he was to see him; and sure he was that he would give money to the priest, and oats to the Pony! And, never could I and Pony pass by a smart lodge and fine white gate, bearing the usual signs of gentility, but he would respectfully turn, and say – 'Dear master, let us call here!'

Brownlow concluded his begging excursion with a successful visit to London.

The Stourbridge chapel was opened in 1823 and was even furnished with an organ, which eventually found its way to Harvington. Sadly, for its builder, it was replaced forty years later by the present church, but Brownlow left Stourbridge for Harvington shortly before Christmas, 1824.[2]

With relief he wrote: 'For me the change was a happy one; calculated to relieve, if not to remove, my painful habitual headaches. Hail, ye rural walks, ye sylvan shades! ye verdant melodious bowers!' but he immediately added ... 'the old moat, full of water too stagnant, cannot be salubrious'. The year after Brownlow's arrival it was noted in the *Laity's Directory* that at Harvington Hall, 'Divine Service on all holidays is at 10 o'clock in the forenoon, and at 3 in the afternoon'. These times remained unchanged until late in the century.

The Harvington mission in the seventeenth century extended over an area of one hundred and forty-four square miles. At the time of John Brownlow's arrival there was to be a drastic re-drawing of its boundaries, since the establishment of the new mission at Stourbridge was followed in 1831 by another at Kidderminster. Brownlow reckoned that this resulted in the reduction of his congregation by some two hundred and thirty persons, chiefly Irish woolcombers, who had come into the district in the eighteenth century. He was clearly aggrieved by the loss, although at the time he ostensibly gave his support to the idea.[3] Indeed the Catholics of Kidderminster, Bewdley, Wolverley, Stourport and Cookley claimed to have been 'left in an extreme state of spiritual destitution' because of ' the nature of their avocation, and the inconvenience of the neighbouring chapel' (i.e. Harvington). Brownlow's feelings were also aggravated by the fact that it was precisely to accommodate the Kidderminster Catholics that Sir George Throckmorton at the instigation of John Marsden had erected the chapel at Harvington which had been opened as recently as Trinity Sunday, 29 May 1825.

Sir George Throckmorton, a semi-permanent invalid, died the following year and was succeeded by his brother, Sir Charles (1757–1840). It is to him that the priests from now on owed their improved accommodation, the late Georgian-style house next to St Mary's Church. Sir Charles proved to be a particularly popular lord of the manor, taking up residence at Coughton, little frequented by his predecessor and even occasionally staying at Harvington. The 7th baronet's portrait at Coughton shows a typical country squire equipped with his dog and gun and belies his interesting background. Besides hunting and shooting, Sir Charles was a philanthropist and natural historian; he even trained as a physician.

The year 1829 saw the long-awaited Catholic Emancipation Bill become law. It also brought Bishop Thomas Walsh to Harvington to confirm thirty-six persons, seven of whom were converts, including Mrs Mary Trafford, the wife of William Trafford of Pleremore.

Trafford himself died in August and was interred 'in a new vault made large enough for four, and situated close by the north side wall, exactly between the two windows nearest the door'.

St Mary's was licensed at Worcester Quarter Sessions in 1839 and then registered for marriages. Until the first year of Queen Victoria's reign marriages had to take place before an Anglican minister to be legal, but Catholics would usually seek to have their marriages blessed by a priest before the Anglican ceremony. Most probably the reason for the absence of marriage records at the Hall before 1804 is fear of contravening the law.

The 1804 marriage took place in the Georgian Chapel at a time when such things were becoming easier. It was followed by six more marriages – that is, up to the time when the Rev John Marsden took charge of the mission. Marsden's ill-health might explain why there is a gap until Brownlow takes over.

Brownlow took a great interest in the Throckmortons and their family history and published his research into their genealogy. Their names and their births and deaths are all carefully noted in his Memoranda. Thus we are told that Sir Charles, the builder of the Priest's House, was succeeded by his nephew, Sir Robert, and that the Hall was the scene of a grand dinner on 1 April 1852 to celebrate the coming of age of Sir Robert's son. Next day there was also a great tea party – perhaps for the estate workers and local Catholics, and even some days afterwards 'a tea drinking for our school children'.

John Brownlow had a succession of housekeepers, although whether they all lived in the house he does not say. There was first his mother; Mary Brownlow was born in 1759 and after the death of her husband came to live with her son at Harvington. She lived into her ninety-fourth year and is buried in the churchyard. She was followed by Mrs Rainford and then in quick succession Martha Fox, Mrs Green and Mrs Yates.

Cheering news came around this time in a letter from Sir Robert Throckmorton, telling Brownlow that his patron would now be raising his salary to £80. On the whole Catholic squires did not pay their chaplains very much, partly because in many cases the landowners themselves were struggling under the disabilities of the penal laws. But perhaps it was on the strength of this rise that Brownlow embarked at this time on the one grand tour of his life. In the congenial company of his friends Dr George Morgan and Canon Jeffries he visited France, Germany, Austria, Switzerland, Bohemia and Belgium. The pleasant experiences of the three clerics are recorded by Brownlow in a large closely-written notebook.

John Brownlow was given to writing poetry as well as researching the history of the Throckmortons and their Hall. A slim volume – one of only forty copies and printed locally contains his sentiments on such subjects as 'My Mother' and the 'Ancient Hall'.[4] The last theme was of course inspired by the increasingly forlorn state of the building in the later years of the nineteenth century; it begins:

*Hail, time-honour'd mansion, esteem'd village queen!*
　*With countenance comely, and dignified mien.*
　*Thy cheek once so youthful, so sprightly, so fair,*
　*Has become sadly furrow'd with age and with care!*
　*And I think I perceive that with grief thou'rt encumber'd,*
　*As if conscious thy days are now few and all number'd!*

If the venerable pile was beginning to look somewhat pathetic it could still provide a picturesque backdrop for a picnic party on a summer afternoon when, as their priest recorded, they 'danced on the green until dusk, then went into the Hall: (they) broke up at 11.0'clock'. In another rustic scene Brownlow tells how he went birds-nesting to Randan Woods one spring; climbing trees after hawks and magpies – 'a youth of only 71'. But perhaps the years were beginning to tell, since Brownlow fell ill in 1869 – an illness that recurred the following year and lasted for six or eight weeks. The expenses involved are duly noted:

| | |
|---|---|
| Dr Fitch | £5. 5. 0 |
| Yates | 1. 0. 0 |
| Betsy | 1. 0. 0 |
| | ——— |
| | 7. 5. 0 |

As he approached eighty the question of retirement was much on his mind. He was worried that Bishop Ullathorne would ask the Throckmorton's steward, Pippet, to insist on his leaving Harvington. But in fact the Bishop made it clear that the old man was welcome to live at the Hall or anywhere else he might wish to be. Unsurprisingly, Brownlow opted to stay on in the Priest's House – an arrangement with which Sir William Throckmorton readily concurred. The future of the mission was now uppermost in the mind of his patron and of Brownlow himself. Sir William's sister, Miss Throckmorton, came over to Harvington to talk things over with Brownlow. After some discussions about the school she went on to suggest that perhaps the mission could be looked after by the Kidderminster priest with a room at the Hall put at his disposal on Sundays. This Brownlow rejected outright since, as he said, with a priest away in Kidderminster, he would be out of touch with his people. Nevertheless, he added: 'She was extremely affable, communicative and kind! having the very best of intentions! God bless her!'

As well as his declining health and the state of the Hall, the strength of the Harvington mission had been affected by the erection of, first, a separate mission in Kidderminster in 1831 and then at Bromsgrove in 1856. From a congregation of three hundred and thirty eight in 1830 Brownlow reckoned that he had merely around two dozen adults and about half a dozen children forty years later. He noted down the following observations:

### Names and Numbers of the Catholics of the Harvington Mission

If you leave out (exclude) the mention of such as may as easily go to Bromsgrove and to Kidderminster respectively, and of such as have the means or facilities to go; as, Warrilow and daughter; Mrs Griffin and two sons; Trafford and family; Askew, wife and daughter; Baylis; Lewis; and perhaps Mrs Harris and two sons, four miles off and from Kidderminster five; and one young man and two old men, three miles off and five miles from Stourbridge: then the other names and numbers will be about as follows:

#### On the Estate of the Lord of the Manor
At the Hall: Mrs Hodson 81 and sister 83, Mrs Morgan 68, Josh Ilsley 67
At Harvington: Corbet, wife and daughter; Pratt 59; widows Rainford 85 and Alpine.
At Chaddesley: Cole 67 and wife.
At Bluntington: Abel (Thos.), Mrs Chare and two daughters

and son (all above thirty years of age). Amounting to ...
16, or 17.

## Not on the Estate

At Harvington: Mrs Turner (here today): Clark and wife
(seldom at Chapel) and their three or four children; Mary
Franks (seldom or never at Chapel) and her two or three children.
At Rushock: Mary Farmer (tepid) and her two or three children (three or four miles off).
If you add Mrs Harris aforesaid and her two children, the
amount of these is, at the most, 18.
Add the said 18 to the aforesaid 17, and the total (unexcluded)
amount of young and old is 35, and that is to say, at the most
about 23 adults and a dozen children: say two dozen adults and
a dozen children (leaving out in this enumeration all those who
live in the extremities of the Mission, and some others, as
explained in the last page).

## Remarks

Mrs Hodson, 81, and John Pratt, 59, are cripples. Elizabeth
Rainford, 85, is blind. The Chares and Abel are five miles
from Kidderminster, the Farmers five miles from Bromsgrove.
About six of the Children, sometimes, come to school (besides
others from the extremities of the Mission)

At the end of May 1875 John Brownlow informed the Bishop that he
intended to retire from pastoral duties in a month's time. Shortly
before then the Bishop called and told him that there would not be a
priest available for Harvington until September. Inevitably the old
man brought up the matter of his annuity, which, he asserted, had
been taken from him by Ullathorne's predecessor, Bishop Walsh, and
given to the Kidderminster Mission. According to Brownlow, some
time after the then patron, Sir Robert Throckmorton, inquired about
the sum of money left by Lady Mary Yate for the Harvington priest
and learned what had become of it. Sir Robert, it seems, intended
writing to the Bishop to insist on its restoration but Brownlow offered
to save him the trouble and wrote instead. Ullathorne never replied.
Chancing to meet Fr Courtney of Kidderminster one day Brownlow
informed him that the annuity would have to be restored to himself.
Courtney then spoke to the Bishop on the subject and as a result Sir

Robert received a letter from Ullathorne in which the Bishop made certain allegations against Brownlow; that the Harvington priest had brought into being the Kidderminster mission and thus adroitly lessened his own care and labour; that not content with a handsome income, he was trying to get for himself some of the charity money which supports the poor priest of the poor mission of Kidderminster. The Bishop concluded by saying that he hoped the patron would frustrate Brownlow's selfish, exorbitant, and cruel cupidity.

In his own Memoranda Brownlow refutes the charges, mentioning his fierce opposition to the setting up of the Kidderminster mission, his contentment with his income, and the fact that it was Sir Robert who, of his own accord, had pressed for the restitution of the annuity. But when Ullathorne, on his visit to Harvington was reminded of the letter to Sir Robert Throckmorton he failed to recall writing it.[5] Their meeting ended with Brownlow offering to say Mass on Sundays until the end of August. But on 23 August the carpenters moved in to pull up the pews in preparation for laying the new floor in the church. The Vicar General, Canon O'Sullivan, also wanted to know what repairs would be needed to the priest's quarters at the Hall in readiness for Brownlow's successor.

On Sunday 26 September the old man managed to say Mass 'with great difficulty, overpowered with grief, feeling it would be my last, yet on 29th Mass again and on Sunday 3rd October I said an early private Mass. Here ended my missionary career!'

That Sunday was, in fact, Rosary Sunday and Canon O'Sullivan returned to celebrate Mass at 10.00 a.m. and to preach. The various repairs in the re-opened church included a new floor and the re-decoration of walls and ceiling, all paid for by Sir William Throckmorton.The congregation at the same time subscribed to a statue of Our Lady which is still here; and the Harvington silver sanctuary lamp was returned from Coughton Court to hang once more before the tabernacle.

Brownlow recorded that

there was an harmonium and good singing by 4 or 5 female voices. The Vicar (General) preached an excellent discourse. In the afternoon was said the rosary, interspersed with admirable remarks and admonitions, and delightful music and singing. There was lastly Benediction. This re-opening of our Chapel after great repairs was like an opening of the heavens to give us a glance of the eternal throne and the glory of the blessed! Praise be to God! Now I am free from pastoral care. Now I must prepare for the joys to come!

John Brownlow gave as the reasons for his resignation – his failing eyesight, his eighty years, and his having been in charge of the Harvington mission for more than fifty years. He was to live for another thirteen years. A final tea party and entertainment was given by some of the congregation in his honour, together with an address read and presented to him by Major William Trafford on 15 November, and some days later the Rev W. H. Wilson arrived to take charge of the mission. John Brownlow's last years are largely a catalogue of ill-health, but there were the occasional visitors and even a trip to his native Lincolnshire. The spring weather tempts him into his orchard where he puts '31 grafts on dwarf apple stock, – 12 "Rose-water Russets" on the north side, and 19 Blenheim Oranges, on the south side'.

On Friday, 9 February 1883, he fell while in the garden and suffered concussion of the spine. His last entry in the memoranda is dated 26 October 1883, when his niece, Mrs Currie of Nottingham, came to see him and stayed the night. He died on 4 March 1888. A list of expenses for the funeral has survived from which we learn that it was attended by the Bishop and fourteen priests. Thirty-two persons sat down to dinner and a dole of bread was given to the poor.[6]

[1] HPA

[2] In the intervening months before Brownlow took up residence William Croskell came to Harvington to help out – although Brownlow makes no mention of this. Croskell from Bulk near Lancaster belonged to a recusant family. He went to Sedgley Park in 1779 and was subsequently sent by Bishop Challoner to St Omer's as church student. From there he proceeded to Douay College, and was imprisoned with its inmates at Dourlens during the French Revolution. After being freed in 1795, Croskell returned to England and being in deacon's orders, was then ordained priest at York along with Dr Lingard. In 1810 he was appointed chaplain to the Bar Convent, served the missions of Linton and Durham and died in 1838 aged seventy. He was grand vicar of the Northern district and was universally respected.
(Gillow, *Biographical Dictionary*, vol. I, pp. 599 – 600.)

[3] Address of the Kidderminster Catholics in the *Catholic Magazine and Review*, vol. II, Feb. 1832, no.13, pp. 206–7. Brownlow appears as first signatory to their appeal for funds to build their chapel, Col I, pp. 124–5, 13 Feb. 1831. In 1830 there was a total of 338 in the Harvington congregation, 213 of whom were Irish and 125 English. The latter were resident in Chaddesley (67) Belbroughton (13) and elsewhere (45). Brownlow asserted later that he attempted to dissuade the Bishop from giving his support to the Kidderminster people, arguing that the recently invented woolcombing machinery would soon arrive in the town and that the combers would be driven away and dispersed, as indeed happened. 'For 20 years the mission became a mere shadow. The body of the people were gone! never, never to return.' For the relief of his impoverished Kidderminster Mission,

Bishop Walsh, many years ago extorted from me an annuity left for the Harvington Mission by Lady Yate' (Memoranda). The outcome of this contentious issue is referred to later. See p. 65.
4  *Poems*. Printed by Thomas Mark, Kidderminster, HPA.
5  A letter from the Rev James McCave of Kidderminster to Canon O'Sullivan dated 31 Jan 1874 (B.A.A. 5352) refers to a confidential conversation between Captain Trafford and himself in which Trafford indicated Brownlow's increasing concern to gather in and retain various amounts of money which were due to him. This concern and other odd traits referred to in a letter may well have been due to a growing sense of uncertainty and insecurity in an old man faced with retirement after more than fifty years in the Harvington mission.
6  HPA.

WILLIAM HENRY WILSON 1875–1883.[1] William Wilson was born in 1837, the son of Henry and Jane Wilson of Douglas Road, Canonbury. A convert to Catholicism, he decided to enter for the priesthood at Oscott. Immediately after ordination he was assigned to Harvington, arriving on 26 November 1875. The little we know about him suggests that he entered into the spirit of the place by encouraging devotion to St John Wall. A letter from the Franciscan convent in Taunton of 12 August 1879 addressed to Wilson indicates that he was begging for a relic of the martyr. The only available one was a very small piece of the spine bone about two inches square.

This was duly despatched to Harvington and incorporated in the mensa of the altar almost a hundred years later. The nuns were delighted to hear that Wilson was intending to commemorate the two hundredth anniversary of St John Wall's martyrdom and hoped that it would spread the knowledge and love of the holy martyrs. A large stone cross with a somewhat crudely carved figure of Christ commemorating the martyrdom was erected in August 1879 in the middle of the churchyard largely owing to the efforts of a young Irish Franciscan. In several issues of *The Universe* in July that year Father Bede Wrigley OFM appealed for subscriptions under the heading, *An English Franciscan Martyr* and asked that subscriptions be sent to the parish priest of Harvington.

On the second centenary of St John Wall's martyrdom, Father Bede blessed the cross in the presence of a large gathering of pilgrims. The Franciscans however were reluctant to support their confrère's appeal, believing the enthusiastic young Irishman to have been influenced by H. T. Galton's historical novel *Gervase Sacheverell* based on the Worcestershire martyr. Wrigley was no scholar but rather a missioner who could pull in the crowds.[2] Inscriptions recording Wall's canonisation have been added in recent years.

In his *Memories and Opinions* Canon William Barry, a literary rector of St Peter's, Leamington, recalls how in his early days as a priest, after some time on the staff at Oscott, he came to take charge at Harvington while Fr Wilson was on sick leave; it is an interesting picture of the mission at that date.[3]

Kept Christmas at Harvington, not without a certain feeling of solitude and freedom ..., Harvington Hall is one of the 'forgotten shrines' to which Dom Bede Camm has devoted some pages in his melancholy book. When I went there dear old Mr Brownlow was still on this side of Lethe, but not living in the Hall; we must bear in mind that the date was 1880, and that he had come to the mission as its priest in 1824. He was a convert from the Church of England, reconciled by a French émigré priest in Lincolnshire.
He had served a wide district year after year, going on Mission every Lent nearly across England. He was learned in varied branches, as, for instance, Botany and also Heraldry, and he knew his Bible well.
The estate of perhaps six thousand acres belonged to Sir William Throckmorton, to whose family it had been left by Lady Yate. The castellated mansion stood on an Islet girt round by a reedy moat, and it had so long been deserted that the highest roofs and attic were in a state of ruin. Otherwise the house was intact ...
My six months at Harvington were the happiest reward save one that ever came to me from our authorities. They brought indeed less than a Curate's ordinary stipend, and God knows how small that is! But, as I felt with a glow of satisfaction, I was henceforth free from a life in the ranks – I mean the rule of existence under which you can never be alone. For that collective life I was not made. Now I could spend the days after my morning Mass without listening for the sound of a bell. I took my walks abroad in the graceful landscape bordering the Severn, lingered in Worcester Cathedral, won some staunch friends like my dear Humphrey Trafford, while recovering an older one, Charles Spink, formerly of Sedgley Park, whose home was not far away from the Hall. This cultivated and amiable man had been tutor in the South Bavarian family of Arco-Vallei, into which Sir John Acton married. He spoke French and German perfectly; and I possess the fine copy of the *Nibelungen Lied* which his pupils at Munich had presented to their English tutor. His daughter was partly brought up in the same circle, so that we formed a snug little German set among ourselves ...

Another old Catholic family named Hailes dwelt at the farmhouse opposite the moated mansion. Their father – who by a singular destiny was born on Christmas Day, and was to die sixty-six years after on the same Festival – farmed most of Sir W. Throckmorton's acres. But my interest in them was heightened by the long association of this family with an English Religious Order founded in exile, know as the 'Dames Anglaises'; and two of its members in succession governed the Convent at Paris no less than forty years ... The second Mother Superior of the Hailes family was yet living; and when I next visited Paris in 1885, I called on her at the English Convent (in Autueil, or Neuilly?) and had a kindly welcome as once taking care of Harvington ...

William Wilson remained at Harvington until 1883, when he retired on sick leave to his maternal home in Haverstock Hill, London, where he continued till two days after his mother's death, at the age of eighty-seven. He himself died on 26 October 1895, aged only fifty-eight.

1 Gillow, CRS vol. 17, p. 370.
2 Justin McLoughlin O.F.M., 'The Franciscans in Worcestershire' *Worcestershire Recusant* 19, June 1972, p. 3.
3 *Memories and Opinions*, G. P. Putnam's Sons, Ltd, London, 1926, pp. 138–44.

CLEMENT ISAAC HARRIS 1883–1900.[1] Clement Harris was born in 1835 at Hamstall Ridware, in Staffordshire. He was educated at Sedgley Park and at Carlow in Ireland. After his ordination to the priesthood in Birmingham on 15 April 1860 he went as assistant to St Austin's, Stafford, to Fr Michael O'Sullivan who later became vicar general to the diocese.

Soon after Fr Harris's arrival the new church was opened and on that occasion Fr O'Sullivan gave credit to his young assistant's part in preparing for this. From Stafford, Harris went on to serve St Anne's, Birmingham and then Tunstall. He was placed in charge of the mission at Harvington in January 1883. Harris had been at Harvington for about five years when he embarked on an enterprising scheme of re-decoration for the church. The work was carried out by Messrs R J Harris and Son of Rugeley, and one wonders if there is a family connection here? Certainly, Fr Harris himself would appear to have possessed artistic talent as he was involved in helping Mr R. J. Hopkins who designed, carried out or supervised the designs for the individual painting. Sadly, these were all painted over along with the stencilling in the sanctuary in the following century and only two of the smaller murals have so far been recently uncovered.[2] Fortunately however, we have the splendid stained-glass window at the east end, which was given by Anne Spink in Fr Harris's time.

The reduction of the congregation in Brownlow's days has already been noted, and this of course led to Harvington becoming a 'Poor Mission', a status it still retains. Not surprisingly then the church notices (which only survive from 1894) frequently allude to the need to increase funds. A typical Sunday collection at this period is £1 1s., although quite often Mr Hailes at the Hall Farm raises the amount by contributing an extra £1.

At Easter 1897 Harris announced gloomily that the offerings are 'not sufficient for cleaning church and flowers – My service of no value whatever'; and at a meeting of the people in the school the previous year the matters addressed were the need to increase contributions for warming the church, keeping the churchyard in order and tuning the organ. The hot water system for heating the building was in dire need of repair and would cost nearly £5.

As the nineteenth century drew to a close so did Fr Harris's tenure of the Harvington Mission. The notices record 'no Mass' and 'sudden illness' in March, 1898 and in the spring of 1900 'Said Mass with great difficulty'. In that year he decided to retire to Kidderminster, where he died on 10 April, 1905, aged sixty-nine. He is buried in St Mary's churchyard at Harvington next to the place he did so much to beautify.

[1] Gillow, CRS vol. 17. From 1900 onwards the sources are Diocesan Yearbook Obituaries, Parish logbooks and other other archive material.

[2] *The Tablet*, December 1888. These two remaining paintings were restored by Sr Bernadette Mewburn Crook RSHM, September 2005.

PHILIP GEORGE ROSKELL 1900–1930. Philip Roskell was born in Liverpool in 1859. After eight years at Oscott and matriculation at London University he went on to complete his studies at the seminary founded by Bishop Ullathorne at Olton. Here he was ordained priest in 1884, and was assigned first to St Peter's, Birmingham, then to Brierley Hill and finally to Harvington in 1900.

The parish numbered some one hundred and twenty at the beginning of the twentieth century. Towards the end of Fr Roskell's ministry it had scarcely increased. A quiet, studious and caring priest, Roskell persevered in what his brethren considered to be the 'lonely, uneventful pastoral life' of Harvington.

Father Philip Roskell, 1902.

A small rural parish easily becomes insular in its outlook, and an amusing anecdote told of the Harvington priest relates how he once rushed to one of his parishioners with the news that 'Something awful has happened, we've got a new family in the parish!' This was later to change and newcomers were welcomed due to the advent of Mary Pedley, wife of Brigadier General Pedley, whose friendly concern for everyone around made her virtually the parish priest's curate.

Early on in his priestly life Philip Roskell took a special interest in the liturgy, which in those days meant rubrics and ceremonial. He was not only the editor of the *Diocesan Ordo* for many years, but was also a diocesan MC, often engaged at functions throughout the diocese. It was here that his abilities in directing important and complicated ecclesiastical ceremonies found ample and congenial scope. In his personal life Roskell was, however, simple in his tastes and habits and had a Lancastrian straight and plain-spoken manner.

Like John Brownlow before him, Roskell's love for his parish comes across in the copious notes on parish life written into one of its registers.[1] The notes commence in 1901 when he celebrated midnight

Mass to inaugurate the new century and continue to within a year of his death. Events on a national scale such as the deaths of 'our venerable and beloved sovereign, Queen Victoria' and that of King Edward VII find a mention, as also the important happenings in the Church at large – the deaths of Leo XIII and Pius X. Episcopal visits for Confirmation at Harvington are recorded, and also the creation of the diocese into an archdiocese with the enthronements and obsequies of its chief pastors.

In 1905 Roskell's predecessor, Clement Harris, died in retirement in Kidderminster and was buried at Harvington. The Bishop and eighteen clergy were present at the Requiem Mass which was celebrated by the Rev Charles Wheatley, parish priest of Kidderminster. In these early years the priest records the gifts made to the church by generous benefactors; Mrs Hailes of the Hall Farm, whose chalice is still used every Sunday, and a handsome carved oak chair donated by Miss Christina Chare, then living at the Hall, also still in use.

By the outbreak of the First World War the school had just closed for want of pupils and the Hall Farm had been let for the first time to a non-Catholic tenant. Other new tenants were occupying the Hall itself and the poor state of the building would eventually cause problems for Roskell when the property passed to the diocese. Given its semi-ruinous state, it was very difficult to reach agreement on a reasonable rent.

The Great War, as it was known, affected every corner of the country and the Harvington parish did not escape. Eighteen men were engaged on active service, one of whom, George Griffin of Rushock, who died at the very end of the war, is commemorated in the churchyard. A brass plate on the organ has the names of other men who also lost their lives; the organ was restored in their memory.

With the end of the war came the end of an era; society began to experience far-reaching changes, as did the parish. Sir William Throckmorton, lord of the manor and patron of St Mary's since 1862, died at Coughton Court on 21 December 1919. His burial took place at Coughton, the chaplains of Coughton, Buckland and Harvington in attendance. For the moment life continued much as before; Christmas revels were held in the Hall with a large gathering of parishioners, an enormous Christmas tree, prizes and entertainment for everyone. 'A truly happy evening, through the great kindness of Mrs. Watts of Sion House'. In the following year the same generous lady gave a stained-glass window to the church. Unusually, this was not a war memorial to lost loved ones but an act of thanksgiving for the safe return of her two sons from the conflict from which so many never came back.

Fr Roskell's next entry of any importance marks a watershed in the history of the parish and the Hall. On 9 November 1923, he notes that

> This Church and the property around it, together with the Old Hall and moat was purchased from the Throckmorton trustees by Mrs Ellen Ferris of King's Norton, and by her presented to the diocese of Birmingham – A noble gift indeed!

However, the sale of the Hall and the Throckmorton estates was to place the parish and its incumbent in an ambiguous situation. Roskell, the last of the Harvington chaplains, was moved to mark the transition with an emotional sermon in which he delicately alludes to the financial difficulties in which the Throckmorton family found themselves:

> It would, I think, ill become me, if I did not at once in all our names, express our sentiments of grateful thanks to all that long line of benefactors, who from our ven. Lady Yate down to the present time, kept the light of faith burning in this district, and so enabled Harvington, as time went on, to become the mother of every Catholic church and parish in the County of Worcester.
>
> Circumstances have now developed, not to be discussed from the altar, which have more or less forced the representatives of the family to part with the property here, and it is our duty to thank God that it has been saved from the desecration that threatened it, and that it has fallen into our own hands, to be preserved and cherished, as a place most sacred and holy for all time. The light of faith, in the fire of divine love has never departed from it all through the days of persecution and devastation; that is the great pride and glory of Harvington, an unbroken chain of priests, perforce humble and retiring, but learned and scholarly, an honour granted to hardly another place in England. That is what makes it what it is, a holy shrine and place of pilgrimage from all parts; firmly planted and watered by the blood of one of God's most blessed martyrs St John Wall. If the Church, the Bride of Christ, lost Harvington she would surely lose one of the most precious jewels she has to show in this spiritually frozen, heretical land of ours.
>
> Now therefore, priest and church are in your care from the 11th of last November, onwards. There is nothing to be obtained for their support except what we can gather from this ground, thinly popu-

lated tho' it be. Certainly we have a small annuity of £21.10s. left by Lady Yate herself, and secured after much difficulty and many forfeitures in the past, as in her day and for many days after nothing could be legally left to a priest . . .

He continued by reminding his congregation that past parishioners had been spoilt by never having been asked to provide such support, and so what he called 'a spirit of little more than a benevolent neutrality' had become deeply rooted in this place, and not unnaturally. The only thing that troubled him was how he was to continue his ministry in this little village without any endowment.

During its long history Harvington had once served a large area, but as each section of this ancient mission had removed itself from the parent home and built churches of their own the mother church was depleted. It did not fall even then, because it had an endowment to support it. He concluded:

We must work and beg to secure a reasonable and permanent endowment. My own near relations are now few, and they have families of their own to support, also churches! My friends, also, owing to my hermit's life for many years, are few, and I see but little of them. But I will do my best, and I trust you will all do the same, and lastly there must be an end at once to benevolent neutrality on the part of the Harvington Catholics.

The Throckmortons may have gone from Harvington, but Sir George's church and Sir Charles's Priest's House would be there for future generations along with the ancient Hall, thanks to the immense generosity of Ellen Grant-Ferris, her family and friends.

In the following year there was once more a gentle but urgent reminder from the pulpit when mentioning seat rents:

Remember what I told you about this last quarter, that though I consider everyone should support the church in this way, yet none of the old members of the congregation are to be disturbed if they don't see their way to help by this offering: of course all of you should see that it is your duty to assist to the best of your power, since the church is now endowed only by what you yourselves provide.

On St George's Day, 23 April 1925, the following letter heralded another milestone in Harvington's history:

The Centenary of St Mary's 1925. From left: Fr Roskell (seated), Bishop of Brentwood, General Pedley and Humphrey Watts.

The Centenary of St Mary's 1925.

We, the Catholics of Harvington, will celebrate the Centenary of our Church in the early summer of this year. The mission of Harvington is old, very old, very sacred and very venerable: indeed it has never been without a resident priest throughout the dark days when to have a priest meant also to have a martyr, and this great honour Harvington possesses in the Venerable Father Wall. We have the names of all our priests for well nigh three hundred years, seventeen in all, an unbroken succession through times ever difficult and perilous, till the permanent Church, built and endowed by Sir George Throckmorton, was opened for public worship on Trinity Sunday, 1825.[2] There are but few Catholic Churches as old as ours, for it was not until years later that the Bill of Emancipation, commonly called the Catholic Relief Bill, was passed into law. We therefore invite the Faithful of the neighbourhood, and all within reach, to come and partake of our joy on Trinity Sunday, June 7th. High Mass at 11. Preacher: The Bishop of Brentwood. The papal Blessing will be given at the end of Mass, Benediction at 4 p.m. The Te Deum will be sung. Garden Party in the grounds of the Old Hall at 4.30 p.m. to meet the Bishop of Brentwood.

(Signed)        Philip Roskell
                Humphrey Watts
                S.H. Pedley

A wire from Rome was received on Saturday, 6 June, through Cardinal Gasparri, conveying the blessings of Pope Pius X1 to parishioners and to all attending the celebration. On the day itself High Mass was sung by Canon Wheatley of St Chad's Cathedral assisted by Fr Walter Hofler of Kidderminster as deacon and Fr William Munster of the London Oratory as subdeacon. Stephen Morris was thurifer and John and Patrick Phair were acolytes.

The Bishop of Brentwood, the Rt Rev Arthur Doubleday, preached to a congregation that packed the church and overflowed into the churchyard. He likewise imparted the papal blessing. The music throughout was sung by the choir of St Ambrose's, Kidderminster, and was greatly appreciated. After Benediction of the Blessed Sacrament, all assembled on the green in front of the Hall where speeches were delivered by Fr Roskell, the Bishop, General Pedley and Mrs Humphrey Watts. The priest commented afterwards with some satisfaction; 'There is little doubt but that we have had the largest concourse of people that ever met together in Harvington throughout its whole history.'

A couple of months later Hardman, Powell & Co. of Birmingham began the work of restoration and redecoration of the church, which was to crown the centenary celebration. Nothing had been done to the walls or roof for over thirty-five years and it was becoming dirty and shabby. The work took seven weeks and the transformation gave great satisfaction to all.

Fr Roskell's final entry is dated 15 December 1929, and appropriately reaches a climax with the beatification by Pope Pius X1 of John Wall, 'priest of this parish and missionary for Worcestershire for twelve years from 1667 to 1679.' To mark this great occasion 'High Mass was sung in this Church by Canon Wheatley of Birmingham Cathedral. After Mass the whole congregation made a pilgrimage to the Hall where Fr Wall had lived so many years (*sic*), and where a shrine had been erected in the Old Chapel to his memory, and there prayers were said.'

The few concluding notes in the register are in another hand and cover the last years of Philip Roskell's ministry. As 1930 and the priest's life drew to a close, visiting priests came to supply during his illness, and it was noted that for the first time for a hundred years there was no Blessed Sacrament in the church.

He retired to St John's house, Droitwich at the end of September after thirty years as a parish priest of Harvington, dying there on 25 November, aged seventy-one.

At his Requiem Mass sung by the canons of the cathedral, his coffin was borne to its resting place in St Mary's churchyard by four friends and neighbours – a sign that during his long ministry here he had endeared himself to all around him; his loveable character is reflected in the words inscribed on his tombstone: *Dulcis anima requiescat in pace!*

[1] BAA P168. Confirmations.
[2] Cf. List of priests according to more recent research pp. 82–3.

ALFRED EDWARD WHITTINGTON 1930–1934. Fr Whittington, born in Warwickshire in 1886, came from a good solid Catholic family. He studied at Oscott and was ordained a priest in 1913.

He was in charge of Wappenbury and the public church of Princethorpe when on 15 September 1930, he received a letter from Archbishop Williams offering him the parish of Harvington.

I rather think that this might be the place for you, at least for a time ... Regarding income, honestly I cannot say what it is worth: prob-

Father Alfred Whittington, 1929.

ably very little: and we may have to make it up from the Poor
Mission Fund. But there is a future for the place, if it is to become,
as I hope and trust it will, a place of pilgrimage and a centre of
devotion to our Martyrs. That is my ambition for it, and if you are
as keenly interested in the project as I am, you may feel that you
would like to have a share in the work ...'[1]

Whittington was evidently taken by the idea and received his appointment immediately.

Philip Roskell was still at Harvington but Whittington found him
very ill indeed. He had been suffering from cancer of the liver for
some months but had lost nothing of his vigorous manner of speech.
The elderly priest did not realise his true state of health and retired to
Droitwich where he died quite peacefully on the morning of 25
November 1931, shortly after his retirement.

Fr Whittington was an energetic man and soon set about
modernising his new home. 'A very disagreeable closet in the garden'
was quickly replaced by a more hygienic contraption, but there was

no inside lavatory or bathroom. The archbishop had been right in thinking that the parish funds were inadequate, for when Whittington arrived the collections averaged £1 5s 0d. There were of course the seat rents (as customary at the time) which produced £15 per annum, together with a few Mass offerings and two small legacies. However, more improvements were rightly deemed necessary, since to begin with the oil lamps in the church had been removed and could not be repaired, and the house was only fitted with two good lamps. Electricity was gradually installed in both church and house and at Midnight Mass of Christmas, 1931, the church was brilliantly lit for the first time. Water was another problem, so the drainage system was overhauled but the supply in the old well in the garden was found to be unfit for drinking. The telephone was introduced in 1931 and a charitable touch, a summerhouse, was erected so that a consumptive young man might live out in the open air. That year the annual fete took £81 12s 6d which helped to boost the Electric Light Fund and even provide a contribution towards the Hall restoration.

On the spiritual side, the parish priest recorded that soon after his arrival in Harvington he had been asked by the dean, Fr O'Keefe of Stourbridge, to take on the Sunday Mass at the little chapel in Clent. Whittington noted that attendance there varied and that sometimes there were less than twenty in the congregation. He gave communion at Harvington at 8.00 a.m., motored to Clent for 8.30 a.m., and returned for 10.45 a.m. at St Mary's. After ten months the strain proved too much for a man whose health was not good and he relinquished this extra duty.

On Easter Day, 1932 the Harvington congregation at 8.30 a.m. numbered seventy adults and five children. At 10.45 a.m. twenty-six adults and six children (twenty-three had already been to the first Mass).

While in the parish, Fr Whittington endeavoured to promote the Harvington Pilgrimage and wrote enthusiastically about it in the *Diocesan Yearbook*. Arousing interest was initially hard work but in time it became an established event in the calendar of the Diocese. He left St Mary's at the beginning of 1934 to serve in Parkfield and Sambourne, dying in 1944.

[1] HPA

JOHN LOVE 1934. John Love commenced his studies for the priesthood after serving in the First World War. He attended the Beda

College in Rome and was ordained in February 1924. He had many moves in the first years of his priestly life, passing quickly from Aston to Snow Hill, Wolverhampton, and on to Cotton as prefect of discipline. In 1928 he was appointed to Cheadle to be curate to the venerable Fr Walter Morris then in his last years. Helping this aged and infirm priest was a very difficult task requiring great delicacy; that he persevered in it for six years proves his patience, tolerance and humility. With this varied experience behind him he came to Harvington as parish priest in 1934 and, after a restful year here he went to Bedworth and finally to Brewood.

Fr Love was a priest of genuine piety and of deep spiritual life, a spiritual life too deep to be stirred by the call of ambition. He was perhaps too reserved to be really well known but it was easy to see that he was devoted to his people. He died in 1961 in his seventieth year.

PATRICK MOORE 1935. Fr Moore arrived in the year of the canonisation of the martyrs, Thomas More and John Fisher, so perhaps it is appropriate that his very brief stay at Harvington is remembered for the pageant which he organised to commemorate that event and in which he took so dramatic a part. The pageant took many weeks of rehearsals for the parishioners and involved young and old. Lady

The Parish Pageant, 1935. Father Patrick Moore is in the background on the left and on horseback, as John Wall.

Mary Yate and a hunted priest (Fr Moore) of course featured, with Fr Moore escaping from the Hall by swimming across the moat! As well as several performances of the pageant the feast of Blessed John Wall (as he then was) was kept on the actual day of his martyrdom with the customary Low Mass at 8.00 a.m. in the Hall Chapel, followed by Solemn High Mass in the presence of the archbishop at 11.00 a.m. in the Hall grounds. On Sunday 10 November Patrick Moore left Harvington to be replaced by a very different kind of man.

CHARLES EDWARD EAGLE 1935–1947. Born in Erdington in 1881, Charles Eagle studied for the priesthood at the English College in Rome and obtained his doctorate in theology at the Gregorian University. He had been in Leek and Warwick before coming to Harvington, where doubtless a country parish suited his scholarly if slightly eccentric character. Doctor (he was always known as that) Eagle was a brilliant writer and had a reputation for writing somewhat mischievous reviews for *The Sower*. Like Fr Roskell he had a deep sense of the English tradition and his spirituality was influenced by the writings of the English mystics. He spent long hours in church,

Rev Dr Charles Eagle.

kneeling at the back, swathed in a voluminous cloak in winter, and deep in prayer. Part of his eccentricity, if it can be believed, was his study walls painted black and relieved only by red velvet curtains. When Eagle first arrived at Harvington he attempted to get the congregation to sing the chants of the Mass; he also refused to preach from behind the iron rood screen erected by Fr Harris. However, towards the end of twelve years, the effort of achieving a higher standard of liturgy had evidently proved too much; the Holy Week services were all said, and on Holy Saturday Dr Eagle and General Pedley conducted everything behind locked doors! Because of his reclusive nature, it has to be said that he failed to appeal to young people in the parish, but among older people, even those outside the Church, he was widely respected.

Eagle's health rapidly declined but he continued with the Sunday services until three days before his end. As he lay dying, May Pedley and other parishioners watched by his bedside. He was buried alongside the church wall but unfortunately his tombstone was later damaged and moved to the outer wall of the churchyard, where his name can just be deciphered. As his obiturist remarked: 'We who knew him as a colleague made full use of his erudition, which was wide as well as deep, for he spoke with authority not only on professional subjects but on English literature and on ecclesiastical art and liturgy.'

JAMES DUNLOP CRICHTON 1948–1955. Born in Birmingham in 1907 James Crichton was educated at Cotton College and Oscott. He was ordained a priest in 1932. Although he did not take a university degree, he nevertheless continued after his ordination to study systematically on his own initiative, researching in the Bodleian and elsewhere, teaching himself languages and covering subjects which seemed to be important to him, especially the history and nature of worship, biblical studies and the Fathers of the Church. He never held an academic appointment, but was much in demand as a visiting speaker at colleges, conferences and summer schools. In this way and through his many publications, he probably exercised more influence than he might have done in an academic institution.

After ordination he was appointed to St Chad's Cathedral, then to Uttoxeter and to Acocks Green. In 1941 he was briefly chaplain to an RAF flying school before moving to Shirley and then to Harvington. Here his interest in the history of the English martyrs and recusants found a congenial climate.

Father James Crichton.

Fr Crichton arrived on the feast of the Epiphany, 1948, together with his housekeeper, Miss Paull and a cat called 'Boss'. He soon discovered that not many parishioners lived in Harvington itself, but with the help of Mrs Pedley, 'who knew everyone and where they lived', he was able to visit most of them. From May to August, as he noted, social life at Harvington could be very vigorous. Cocktail parties on lawns abounded!

In the village there were two or three old families, and in Lady Yate's almshouses in the lane approaching the Hall there was a delightful Mrs Elwell belonging to one of these families. She was then in her late seventies. In the other villages the new priest found that most of the residents were middle class and came from elsewhere, a flock of around two hundred in all.

In the parish there were other communities. At Mustow Green there was a hostel with one hundred and ten Poles, former soldiers, most of whom had with great difficulty and much suffering, joined General Anders' army in Soviet Russia. Crichton knew no Polish and not surprisingly found them rather reserved. Later they were given their own chaplain and eventually their own church in Kidderminster which still exists.

A second hostel further away at Summerfield housed a mixed collection of people, Irish and others, who came to St Mary's so that it was overflowing. Every seat was occupied and there was standing room only in the large porch. This hostel also closed and became a teachers' training college. It provided a one year course for ex-servicemen who wanted to enter the teaching profession.

Thirdly, at the end of the Second World War a preparatory school known as Penryn School transferred from Edgbaston to Winterfold House near Harvington. The headmaster of this boarding school for boys was Hugh Arbuthnott. Hugh's three brothers were priests, and his wife, Janet, was a convert to Catholicism. They had eight children, but Janet took a very active part in parish life and is remembered as the founder of the annual Harvington festival of music and drama. At Hugh Arbuthnott's request Fr Crichton undertook to give three classes in religion at the school every Friday morning, while Janet instructed the children in preparation for First Communion.

Finally, there was the Hall, where it was expected that the parish priest would naturally be a member of the Management Committee.[1] Unfortunately Archbishop Masterson's appointment of James Crichton as chairman of the Committee was to lead to the priest's transfer against his wishes to another parish. All in all there was enough and more than enough to do, but the first care had to be the parish. The income was small and after Fr Crichton had been there a few months the diocese withdrew the subsidy it had been paying the Harvington priests, on the grounds, perhaps, that the school would increase their chaplain's income. Crichton now turned his attention to the church which was in need of refurbishment, so we find him asking for a frequent special collection to meet the costs of what he had in mind. This not only meant repairs and re-decoration but involved a far more drastic scheme for the whole building. Between 1949 and 1953 Fr Harris's iron screen was removed entirely, and with a handsome donation from Mrs Ethel Watts the Victorian stencilling of the sanctuary, which was said to have been affected by damp, was replaced by oak panelling around the lower part of the walls. In place of Dr Eagles's riddle curtains and reredos a fine new carved reredos with figures of St Oswald and St Wulstan was installed; the lower part of the east window which had only plain glass panels was also filled with figures of the martyrs, to be completed at a later date with fleur-de-lys designs. The sacristy was to become a Lady Chapel and a new sacristy built. The font was to be removed to the outer porch and new oak benches provided for the congregation. Stations of the Cross carved in stone and in low relief were to replace the existing oleographs.

Carrying on the tradition of devotion to the Harvington martyr, Fr Crichton placed an imaginary painting of John Wall, together with a locked casket containing his breviary, in the blocked window nearest the altar, installed new lighting and restored the organ.

After the late Victorian exuberance the church must have presented a dramatic simplicity, but it is to be regretted that by overpainting all the previous murals a certain amount of high quality work was lost to view. (Two of the sanctuary paintings were once more exposed in the course of the 2003 re-decoration of the church.) Not all Crichton's plans, however, were carried out; doubtless lack of funds prevented the building of a new sacristy and the provision of new seating and the carved stone Stations of the Cross.

In Dr Eagle's last years the church services were greatly reduced and a sung Mass was unknown. Soon after Crichton's arrival in the parish he appealed for volunteers to form a choir and from then onwards there was a weekly choir practice. The choir was composed of a small group of adults and also boys from Winterfold School who were instructed in the niceties of plainsong by their enthusiastic priest. The congregation, too, was soon encouraged to join in, and so the liturgy was once more brought back to life. A further and popular innovation was a carol service which became an annual event at the end of the Christmas term.

Not content to revive the music of the Mass, Crichton also trained the Winterfold boys to serve in the sanctuary; he was also pleased to find that a twelve-year-old could be a perfectly efficient master of ceremonies for a sung Mass.

In all this he showed himself to be the pastor as well as the liturgist, finding time for parish duties as well as for his work as editor of *Liturgy*, the periodical of the Society of St Gregory (a position that he held from 1952–1970). In innumerable talks and lectures up and down the country and the sheer volume of his writings he inspired all who came with his vision and understanding of the liturgy. Clearly a progressive in liturgical matters, he was viewed with suspicion for many years by the more conservative church authorities until, that is, the floodgates were opened in the post-Vatican II period when he came into his own as an exponent of 'the changes'. This belongs to the time after he left Harvington, but it should be noted here that in 1980 he was appointed a Prelate of Honour at the request of the Bishops' Conference of England and

Wales; and, again, at the same Conference's request, in 1992 he was awarded an Honorary Doctorate by the Pontifical Liturgical Institute of Sant'Anselmo.

In 1953, the Chairman of the Harvington Management Committee, Fr Warner,[2] resigned and the archbishop appointed Fr Crichton in his place; it was a position he was reluctant to accept, anticipating a conflict of interest between the parish and the Hall. At that time the association called 'The Friends of Harvington Hall' had representatives on the Management Committee who were elected at an annual general meeting. Differences of opinion between the then curator, Veronica Webster, who was assisted by her husband, Lionel, and the Committee, had been apparent for some time and now came to a head. Briefly, the problems amounted to inadequate staffing and facilities and the domination of the committee by H. R. Hodgkinson after his official retirement in 1953 aged eighty-one. In spite of Fr Crichton's efforts to pour oil on troubled waters, the atmosphere at the summer AGM of 1955 which was packed with the curator's supporters called for immediate action. Archbishop Grimshaw dissolved the committee forthwith and formed a new and smaller one composed almost entirely of his priests; the curator's employment was eventually terminated and the Friends disbanded. A few weeks later Crichton, who had already been offered the parish of Uttoxeter and turned it down, (he once described it as 'an ecclesiastical wilderness') was peremptorily ordered to Pershore. In this attractive old town with its beautiful remains of a Benedictine abbey church the Catholic church now had merely a tin hut and not much else for this ardent liturgical scholar. His announcement at Mass on his last Sunday in Harvington was understandably bleak: 'The Archbishop has moved me from here and appointed me to Pershore – I leave on Thursday. Fr Bagnall will come here as parish priest.' In the event James Crichton spent thirty happy years at Pershore, building his 'dream church' and dying there in 2001 at the ripe old age of ninety-four.

[1]  HHA and Crichton papers, BAA.
[2]  Then at Besford Court, Worcestershire.


THOMAS VINCENT BAGNALL 1955–1968. At heart Fr Bagnall was so much of a countryman that few would guess that he was born and had spent a good deal of his life in Handsworth, Birmingham. He served in the First World War, having enlisted in the Norfolks, and saw active service in France where he received shrapnel wounds in

Father Thomas Bagnall.

the legs; and it was while in the army that he felt his first promptings to study for the priesthood, very largely through the example of the well-known Jesuit priest, Fr William Doyle, a chaplain. After demobilisation Bagnall returned for a while to his pre-war occupation, but in 1929 he finally decided to pursue a priestly vocation with the encouragement of Archbishop Williams who sent him to the Beda College in Rome. After ordination he served as a curate in Fenton and Uttoxeter. In 1936 he became parish priest of Blackmore Park, and a year later he was transferred to Wolstanton, where he remained throughout the Second World War. After a return to Blackmore Park and some two years of ill-health, (he suffered from TB) he served at Atherstone and finally at Harvington.

Fr Bagnall, popularly know as 'The Bag' was a good mixer, socially-minded, and a great believer in parish guilds. He saw the guilds as a means of promoting and harnessing together the spiritual and material potentialities of his people perhaps with greater effectiveness than is possible with the modern parish council. He had the reputation for being kind-hearted and generous in the extreme, and more than once his housekeeper found at the last minute that the weekend joint had been given away! He reckoned that he was no Latinist or liturgist and certainly no intellectual, although he pretended to remain in the background; he was a real priest of the people, who knew how to share in their joy and sorrows.

In 1968 he retired to Hartlebury in a bungalow which he named 'St Cajetan' where he continued to give help to the local priests. Very sadly, he died on 25 May 1973, as a result of a road accident at the Mitre Oak, Hartlebury.

LAURENCE WALLACE JONES 1969–1975. Laurence Jones came from Edgbaston and was educated at Cotton College where he soon showed signs of the brilliance and application which were to mark his academic career.[1] After higher studies at Birmingham Technical College where he obtained a London University BSc. Engineering with honours, he was accepted for Oscott. Having spent just one term there he was sent to the English College, Rome, for his Doctorate in Philosophy and Theology, winning golden opinions from his mentors. He was ordained priest at St John Lateran at Easter 1929.

Rev Dr Wallace Jones.

His first appointment was at Gravelly Hill, Erdington, after which he taught a wide variety of subjects at Cotton College for many years. He was then appointed parish priest of St Mary Immaculate, Warwick, where he stayed for six years. From Warwick he went to St Austin's, Stafford, and after thirteen years there he came to Harvington. Surprisingly, parishioners found this popular schoolmaster priest very reserved in spite of his announcement on arrival that he wished to be known as 'Father' rather than 'Doctor' Wallace Jones. It was generally acknowledged that he gave splendid sermons, and as someone said, 'as a parish we grew up from him – we always learnt.' He was also much in demand as a preacher on ecumenical occasions in the locality.

The move to Harvington, however, was occasioned by Jones's rather advanced views and practices, and in fact it was here that he became 'unstuck' on the issue of intercommunion. Nevertheless, he won the hearts of his people and well suited this parish with his love of the English martyrs and the countryside. The picture of this country priest can be complemented with these other small details: Wallace Jones, often unshaven, smoking a pipe and accompanied by his greatly loved Collie dog Brecon, going off in search of fungi on which he was also something of an expert!

In 1975 Jones's housekeeper retired to live in Chaddesley Corbett and he himself decided that the time had come for retirement. He went first to live with his sister in Formby, Lancashire, and then, after her death, he moved to Aston Hall, Staffordshire where he died in 1993. His funeral took place in St Mary's, Harvington, on a beautiful June day. He had requested only wild flowers to decorate the church which looked especially lovely filled with all his favourite flowers. His ashes were buried in the churchyard and an oak form was later placed in the church in his memory.

[1] Jones's ability can be seen in the poem entitled 'The Memorial' published in *The Cottonian* vol. x, midsummer, 1920 No. 1 when a member of the Upper Fifth at Cotton.

### The Memorial
*When three full weeks of joyous May had flown,*
*And to the earth the warm spring sun had shown*
*His sweetest smiles, and flower and bird and beast*
*Were joined in welcoming the Spirit's feast,*
*Then raised they up to those immortal Dead*

*Who for their Country's sake their blood had shed,*
*A simple cross of oak with base of white,*
*A tribute to their Faith and Courage bright.*
*Unto the Church they hied them there to pray.*
*The Mass was said, and thence they took their way*
*With solemn chant to bless the honoured cross*
*Commemorating gain of life, not loss.*
*They stand not there to call back thoughts of War,*
*Of havoc, of distress, of fields afar,*
*But they those noble souls do reverence*
*Whose valour gained no earthly recompense.*
*They won no mortal cross on breast to wear,*
*Nor glorious wreath of fame, nor laurel fair,*
*Naught but a wooden cross at head of grave,*
*The only sign a grateful nation gave*
*To these her sons, who dying, kept her free*
*From tyranny and dreadful slavery.*
*Their cross the same as that on which Our Lord*
*Through bitter death did us, His servants, ward*
*From all dangers that beset this life*
*Where evil shows its head, and sin is rife.*
*Their sacrifice the same and best of all*
*That in this human life can us befall.*
*For when He walked this earth He oft did say*
*That none so loving, none so brave as they*
*Who for a fellow-man their lives do give,*
*For they, through dying now, henceforth should live.*
*Such are thy sons, St. Wilfrid, Patron dear!*
*And thou their deeds dost ever love to hear.*
*Oh, may we serve our God as well as they,*
*To whom we thus a loving tribute pay.*

JOSEPH LACY 1975–1978. Joseph Lacy was born in Drumlish, County Longford, Ireland, in 1925. His appointment to Harvington, a place so intimately bound up with the history of English Catholicism was perhaps therefore surprising. Indeed, his first assignment after ordination to the priesthood back in Ireland was to that very Irish parish of St Patrick's, Dudley Road, Birmingham.

In 1963 he became parish priest of Lower Gornal where he is remembered for having built a parish club, a church and a presbytery all within a very short time. He was not, however, destined to enjoy

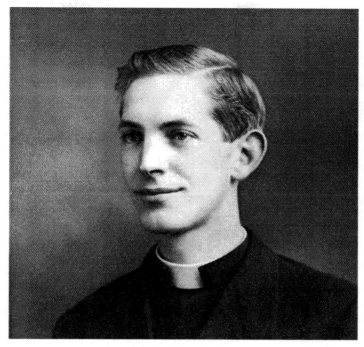

Father Joseph Lacy.

the fruits of his labours for long, for the recurrence of a kidney complaint which he had in earlier life resulted in renal failure and having to give up parish work. Yet, after being carefully nursed back to a reasonable state of health by the Sisters of the Holy Trinity Convent, Kidderminster, he was once again made parish priest this time at Harvington.

With his customary dynamism where building projects were concerned, Lacy was soon telling his congregation that 1975, the one hundred and fiftieth anniversary of the opening of St Mary's, ought to be marked in some suitable way, and he would propose a new and permanent altar facing the people together with the consecration of the church. The church was not in fact consecrated until Archbishop Couve de Murville came in 1985. Carmel Cauchi, a Maltese artist, popular at the time, was presently asked to make sketches and the priest himself begged to be allowed the great privilege of bearing the lions' share of the cost, assuring the people 'This is no blarney!' Archbishop Dwyer was then approached for this approval, but

His Grace seemed to be more interested in the keeping of parish accounts. I agreed that, whereas in the past I had not bothered, I would now keep proper accounts. His Grace then threatened me as follows: 'If you do not keep accurate accounts I will take it as proof that you are not equal to the job of looking after Harvington.' I left his presence, distressed and depressed and, later on I was sick ... I think he is more ill than even he suspects [Dwyer retired in 1981]. Meanwhile the altar will be erected, in one form or another, and the church will be consecrated, and thank God I feel confident that I am equal to the task for which I have come here.[1]

Approval for the altar did at last come early in the following year. It was to be of reinforced concrete, faced with ceramics and would cost £750. For the front Cauchi designed a pietà, and the parish priest was delighted with the transformation of the sanctuary. Outside the church he also erected a statue of Our Lady of Lourdes, purchased for £20 from the former St Gilbert's School in Hartlebury when the De la Salle Brothers left the area.

In January 1976, Lacy commented that 'the worst storm of the century' uprooted trees throughout the Midlands and damaged the church and Hall roofs. To cover the cost of repairs, principally the Priest's House which needed attention to the roof and re-decorating, he obtained permission to send all the paintings in the house to Lock and England's, Leamington, for auction, opining that there was only one picture of value which was a *Procession of the Pietà* in some Italian town by the Belgian artist Unterbergen.

Joe Lacy was fond of an argument but would deny that he was argumentative. He hated ostentation. At times he could be devastating in his criticism of some of the changes in the liturgy or in the Church's discipline; he nevertheless could be extremely 'laid back' and was known on one occasion to have absented himself from a Confirmation service at Harvington at which Archbishop Dwyer presided. No one knew where the parish priest had gone!

[1] HPA

GEOFFREY ROBERT TUCKER 1978–1999. Geoffrey Tucker was born in 1919 in Ashbury in Berkshire and came from farming stock. His father (a Baptist, later an Anglican) died when Geoffrey was five and his mother (also an Anglican) was left with the daunting task of bringing up a family of seven. Together with his brothers, Geoffrey attended Shaftsbury Grammar School and on leaving was articled to the borough surveyor of Reading. His training, however, was interrupted by the outbreak of the Second World War and his enlistment in the Royal Engineers. After demobilisation he read French language and literature at Oxford, and it was through his contact with the Dominicans at Blackfriars that he eventually asked to be received into the Catholic Church.

Later Geoffrey spent a year in France teaching at a lycée in Clermont-Ferrand and found his way to the shrine of Our Lady of Oricival in the Auvergne. It was here, he asserted, that he felt the call to the priesthood. On leaving Oxford he went to the Beda College in Rome and was ordained for the Archdiocese of Birmingham in 1955.

In 1957 Father Tucker became the first full-time Catholic chaplain at Birmingham University and set about building the chaplaincy at Newman House in Edgbaston. The hospitality he offered there to the student community was legendary. In the early sixties Tucker was appointed Catholic advisor to the independent television company in the Midlands and remained successively with ABC, ATV and Central, becoming the longest-serving Catholic advisor to any television

Father Geoffrey Tucker.

company in the country. This involvement with television brought him in turn into the wider field of international religious broadcasting.

Geoffrey Tucker was a very charismatic figure with a wonderful ability to communicate and a capacity for friendship, especially in the higher echelons of society. His ministry at Harvington to which he came after the parishes of Chasetown and Headington is largely remembered for the tradition of hospitality begun at the university chaplaincy and extended in the parish to his wide circle of friends and others. He was always keen to invite people to visit or to share a meal, although it was the company and conversation that mattered most. Tucker's hospitality amounted to an open-house policy in which many people with 'issues' were made welcome, often at his cost, both financial and emotional, but he simply saw this as 'what one should do'. Although a convert, and unsympathetic to traditionalists, Tucker became engrossed in the Hall and its association with the penal days, which, perhaps, was partly responsible for his election to the Old Brotherhood of the Secular Clergy. The ongoing restoration and maintenance of Harvington Hall were his particular concerns, as was indeed the Festival which he and Janet Arbuthnott, the parish organist, founded originally to promote early music and drama.

In the day-to-day running of the parish, Tucker sought more involvement of the laity and various committees were set up with a view to the future when the shortage of clergy might necessitate parishioners having to cope with the more mundane tasks.

During Geoffrey Tucker's time at Harvington, a few improvements were made to the property. The Stable (as it was known) was rebuilt following its partial destruction by fire, and became a modest parish meeting room; and in the Priest's House a much-needed new heating system was installed. Tucker otherwise took little interest in his surroundings and preferred to be out and about and especially to travel abroad. His later years, however, were marked by much pain and illness, although he kept most of this to himself and struggled to keep up his usual activities, including foreign travel. Having achieved his eightieth birthday and completed over twenty years as parish priest here, he suffered a stroke and died on 21 June 1999. The fact that so many friends and acquaintances, including several Anglican dignitaries, attended his Requiem Mass at St Chad's Cathedral was a tribute to Geoffrey Tucker's concern for ecumenism.

**DAVID ANTHONY HIGHAM 1999–.** Following a somewhat unusual path, I came to Harvington after many years of monastic life.

Harvington Hall with St Mary's Church and the Priest's House (left) and
The Hall Farm (right), 2002.

Humphrey Pakington, 1599 by Cornelius Jonson.

Abigail Pakington, 1630 by Cornelius Jonson.

Dame Mary Yate, *c.*1660.

Apollonia Yate.

Sir Robert Throckmorton by Nicholas de Largillière.

Sir George Throckmorton.

Sir John Courtenay Throckmorton.

Sir Charles Throckmorton.

Sir William Throckmorton.

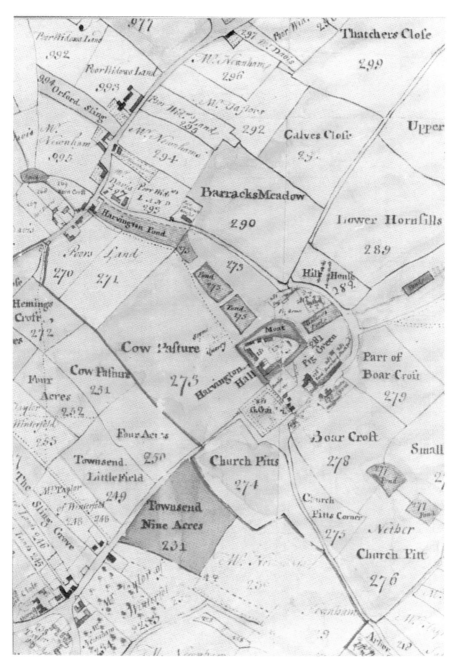

Part of the estate map of 1745–1746 by Thomas Thorp, showing The Great Garden of the Hall and Farm buildings formerly on the site of St Mary's Church.

St Mary's Church: the exterior.

St Mary's Church: the interior, 2006.

The Priest's House: the Study, 2006.

The Georgian Chapel, Harvington Hall, 1743, after the restoration of 1986.

St Mary's Church: interior, 2006.

Although my family backround was closely linked to the Dominicans – they ran our parish and I attended their schools – nevertheless, I decided to enter the Benedictine Order at Prinknash Abbey, Gloucester, in 1944. With the post-war expansion of that community, I was among a small group of monks who were then sent to re-populate St Michael's Abbey, Farnborough, Hampshire, formerly a monastery of French origin founded by the exiled Empress Eugénie, widow of Napoleon III, and now staffed by a diminishing number of monks from the Abbey of Solesmes.

Ordained priest in 1954, I was eventually appointed superior and, in due course, elected conventual prior when the community attained autonomy in 1980. Not long after, Bishop Emery of Portsmouth asked us to take charge of the largest parish in the town, and for three years I combined the duties of prior with those of parish priest of 'Our Lady of Lourdes', Cove, Farnborough.

On relinquishing the office of prior ten years later, I returned to the Midlands to become chaplain to the Benedictine nuns at Oulton near Stone, Staffordshire, and to be, briefly, the superior of a small monastic community at Alton nearby. From Alton I went on to join the team running the combined parishes of Cheadle, Alton and Cotton, and to join the Archdiocese of Birmingham. In 1999 I exchanged the largely rural Staffordshire Moorlands for St Chad's Cathedral in Birmingham's inner city. It was fortunate that, with my love of the countryside, I was soon offered the parish of Harvington.

In this small country parish I found a thriving and welcoming congregation, but a church and presbytery in need of sympathetic restoration. Initially, I set about getting to know the parishioners and starting work on the property. Several months were spent in restoring the Georgian-style house to a more appropriate appearance. Over many years and with the coming and going of priests, structural changes had been made to the building, and original furnishings of interest had, in some cases, unfortunately disappeared.

With Harvington's long history, I had hoped for more in the way of archives, but at least a small quantity of records survived while others had been transferred to the diocesan archives. The parish also retained a quantity of books left by previous incumbents, which have now been more suitable housed in the Study. Surviving historic records have also been carefully documented and additional material is continually being sought, so as to build up a more complete picture of the parish.

For company, I share the house with a border collie and two

Father David Higham.

Burmese cats, who manage to live together more peacefully than some humans I have known.

In 2003 the roof and walls of the church were repaired followed by the re-decoration of the interior. A new lighting and sound system were installed at the same time. Other refurbishments included improved fittings for the reredos and tabernacle, a brass eagle lectern and new oak seating. Archbishop Vincent Nichols came to bless Gabrielle Mercer's impressive sculpture of St John Wall, and two years later a stained-glass window was installed behind the font, which previously had been rescued from the garden. Outside the church a new stone pathway has been laid, almost completing the programme of restoration.

An occasion of special thanksgiving and joy was my Golden Jubilee of Priestly Ordination in 2004, celebrated with Archbishop Vincent Nichols and many clergy, family, parishioners and friends. I have indeed much for which to be grateful.

## PRIESTS OF HARVINGTON

| | |
|---|---|
| c.1603–1613 | Samuel Smallman |
| c.1642–1653 | Humphrey Lutley |
| c.1661 | Michael Gennings |
| 1664 | Thomas Catterall |
| 1671–1678 | John Wall |
| 1686–1687 | Sylvester Jenks |
| c.1692–c.1697 | William Harris |
| c.1703 | John Morgan |
| 1712–1714 | Robert Heydon |
| 1714–1726 | William Thompson |
| 1722–1739 | Charles Dodd |
| 1739–1743 | Thomas Atherton |
| 1743–1750 | Charles Fitzwilliam |
| 1750–1751 | James Layfield |
| 1750–1752 | George Bishop |
| 1752–1792 | Arthur Vaughan |
| 1792–1803 | Richard Cornthwaite |
| 1803–1806 | George Hartley |
| 1806–1816 | John Corne |
| 1816–1824 | John Marsden |
| 1824–1875 | John Thomas Brownlow |
| 1875–1883 | William Henry Wilson |
| 1883–1900 | Clement Isaac Harris |
| 1900–1930 | Philip George Roskell |
| 1930–1934 | Alfred Edward Whittington |
| 1934–1935 | John Love |
| 1935 | Patrick Moore |
| 1935–1948 | Charles Eagle |
| 1948–1955 | James Dunlop Crichton |
| 1955–1969 | Thomas Vincent Bagnall |
| 1969–1975 | Laurence Wallace Jones |
| 1975–1978 | Joseph Lacy |
| 1978–1999 | Geoffrey Robert Tucker |
| 1999– | David Anthony Higham |

# 7

# THE LORDS OF THE MANOR

## THE PAKINGTONS

It is to the Pakingtons and the Throckmortons that Harvington owes the establishment and continuation into modern times of the Catholic mission here. Father Faber, writing of those times in the heady years of the post-Emancipation Catholic revival, spoke only too truly of the 'Faith of our fathers, living still in spite of dungeon, fire (a long-standing misprint for the more accurate 'fine') and sword'. But it was precisely because such families were in a better financial position than humbler folk that many of them were able to cling on to their faith. Nevertheless, their situation must often have been precarious and the self-sacrifice involved extreme.

The Harvington Pakingtons had their roots in Worcestershire where Humphrey Pakington was born c.1495 at Stanford-on-Teme.[1] Through their connection with the Mercers' Company and the Bar in London they gradually acquired considerable lands in their own county, in Herefordshire and Shropshire, as well as properties in London. Humphrey's second son, John, inherited the manor of Chaddesley Corbett among other lands from his uncle, Sir John Pakington, Justice of the Great Session in Wales. John married Elizabeth Newport and predeceased her by some years. It was she, therefore, who as a widow, Mistress Pakington, was reported to the authorities for allowing the elderly Massing priest, John Felton, to officiate at her house in Chaddesley Corbett. Our Humphrey (the third of that name) the son of John and Elizabeth, was educated at Shrewsbury School. Born in 1555, he was to suffer massive fines for his recusancy, having two-thirds of his estates sequestered for sixteen years. In 1601 or 1602 he married Lady Bridget Norris, daughter of Sir Thomas Kingsmill, High Sheriff of Hampshire and widow of Sir Thomas Munster,

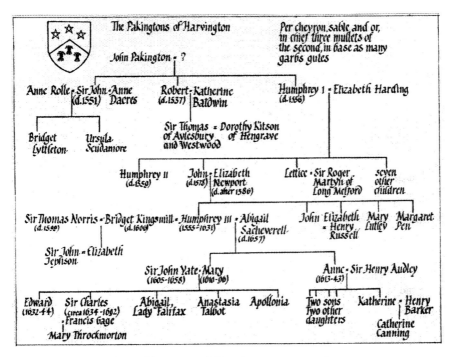

The Pakingtons of Harvington – genealogy.

Ireland. Bridget died five years later and Humphrey remarried soon after. His second wife was Abigail, daughter of Henry Sacheverell of Morley, Derbyshire. They had four children; two died in infancy, but the sisters, Mary, baptised at St Cassian's in Chaddesley on 20 November 1610 and Anne, who was baptised there three years later. On them were settled respectively the Worcestershire and Shropshire estates.

After the death of Humphrey, Abigail was fined for recusancy – a wife could not be fined while her husband was alive. Like many Catholics Abigail espoused the King's cause in the Civil Wars, and we read of her volunteering a horse for the Royalist army and being noted among the 'Delinquents' who deserved to have their estates confiscated by Parliament.

Anne Pakington married Sir Henry Audley of Berechurch, Essex, in 1628. Again her husband incurred fines and other penalties for his Catholic faith. His grandmother was a relative of the Jesuit martyr and poet, St Robert Southwell. Anne died at Harvington Hall in 1642 in

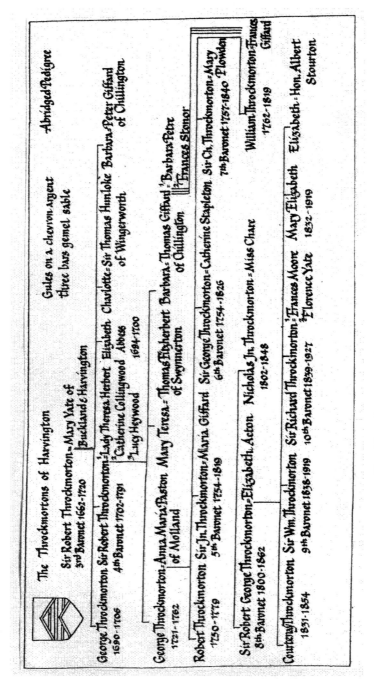

The Throckmortons of Harvington – genealogy.

the same year in which the Puritan mob burnt down the family home in Essex.

Mary, the elder daughter of Humphrey and Abigail, married Sir John Yate of Buckland in Berkshire, a relative of the Yates of Lyford where St Edmund Campion was captured. Sir John was charged with recusancy in London in 1632 and gave his address as Chaddesley Corbett. In 1651 his estates were sequestered because of his loyalty to the king. Having said this, it would seem that the rest of the family were less affected financially, for Lady Mary Yate had considerable means with which to support her religious and charitable purposes. The five children of the marriage made links with other notable Catholic families – with the Gages of Firle Place in Sussex, the Fair-faxes of Gilling Castle in Yorkshire and the Talbots of Longford in Shropshire. One daughter Apollonia, did not marry, and was mentioned as a recusant in Longford. She dutifully erected the monument to her mother in St Cassian's.[2]

Lady Yate's son, Charles, predeceased her, so that at her death in 1696 Harvington passed to his daughter, another Mary Yate, who married Sir Robert Throckmorton of Weston Underwood, Buckinghamshire and Coughton Court, Warwickshire.

[1] Lionel and Veronica Webster, 'The Pakingtons of Harvington', *Recusant History* 12, no. 5, April 1974, pp. 203–15.
[2] Appendix II, pp. 170–171.

## THE THROCKMORTONS

It has been remarked that 'because Coughton Court has been associated with the Throckmortons ever since 1409, it is easy to think of them as living only twenty miles from Harvington and riding over regularly on estate business for two hundred years, as son succeeded father in the baronetcy.'[1] In actual fact their visits to Harvington were very infrequent and they seldom stayed in the Hall and then only briefly. Secondly, at no time between 1696 and 1923 did the Throckmorton baronetcy pass from father to son. The family took its name from a small village of that name near Fladbury in Worcestershire.

The founder of the dynasty, John, married a wealthy heiress, Eleanor Spiney, which gradually enabled the Throckmortons to acquire the lands of Coughton, near Studley. Further advantageous unions brought them Weston Underwood in Buckinghamshire (15th century), Buckland in Berkshire and Harvington in Worcestershire (17th century) and Molland in Devon (18th century). Sir George Throckmorton, who became lord of Coughton in 1519, was an outspoken opponent of Henry VIII's divorce from Catherine of Aragon, and although he supported the suppression of the Pilgrimage of Grace, he steadfastly refused to accept the king's changes in religion and was imprisoned for a time in the Tower of London. From Sir George's family of eight sons and eleven daughters were descended a friend of Mary, Queen of Scots, two traitors in Elizabeth I's reign, and some of the Gunpowder Plotters. Most of the Throckmortons followed Sir George in their loyalty to the Old Faith and married Catholics, while some branches conformed to Protestantism to a greater or lesser extent. Coughton was one of the earliest recusant houses and sheltered Catholic priests, notably the Jesuits, Garnet and Tesimond, together with the laybrother and builder of hides, Nicholas Owen. As Catholics, the Throckmortons were now consigned to leading their lives away from national prominence, forfeiting the opportunity of gaining high titles and honours.

Nevertheless, the need of Charles I to raise money in his growing struggle with Parliament brought Sir Robert Throckmorton (d.1650) a baronetcy in 1642.

### Sir Robert Throckmorton, 3rd baronet (1662–1720)

Grandson of Sir Robert Throckmorton (d.1650), married Mary, daughter of Sir Charles and Lady Frances Yate. It was this marriage that led to the family acquiring the considerable estates of Buckland and Harvington.

In the early eighteenth century Sir Robert reduced the Hall to little more than half its original size by demolishing a good part of the building.

### Sir Robert Throckmorton, 4th baronet (1702–1791)

His portrait by Largillière hangs in the Drawing Room at Coughton, held the title for seventy-one years. He married three times in the course of his very long life, and at his death was buried in the tomb in the centre of the old church at Coughton intended for an early sixteenth-century ancestor but never used. The splendour of Largillière's portrait is appropriate for a man who spent extravagantly on the re-building of Buckland and extensive renovations at Coughton. Sir Robert was responsible for constructing the modest 'Georgian Chapel' in the grounds of Harvington Hall in 1742. It is also likely that he maintained chapels in his other houses, though doubtless more comfortably furnished. His grandchildren, the 5th, 6th and 7th baronets, all brothers, succeeded to the title in a fairly short space of time.

## Sir John Courtenay Throckmorton, 5th baronet (1754–1819)

Together with his brothers, Sir John was educated by the Benedictine monks of St Gregory's, Douay. In 1782 he married Mary Catherine, daughter of Thomas Giffard of Chillington, by his first wife, Barbara, daughter of Robert, Lord Petre. On the death of his grandfather, John and his wife moved from Weston Underwood to Buckland. Harvington's lord of the manor is one of the more interesting later Throckmortons since he was actively involved in the process leading up to Catholic Emancipation. Sadly, he died before that was finally achieved.

A member of a small group of representatives of old Catholic families called the Catholic Committee, Sir John, his chaplain at Buckland, Joseph Berington, and others were assiduous in promoting the full acceptance of Catholics by their fellow Protestant countrymen. They claimed that Henry VIII's Oath of Supremacy had been misinterpreted by Catholics, and that, if rightly understood, it was not incompatible with Catholic principles. The Committee while recognising the authority of the Pope in matters of doctrine, believed that Catholic bishops should be elected in England and subject to a Government veto. Sir John Throckmorton published three Letters *addressed to the Catholic Clergy of England on the appointment of bishops* which appeared between 1790 and 1792. They were attacked by Bishop Milner in his usual intemperate manner, although the quickening pace of toleration, including the repeal of the recusancy laws, freedom of worship, and negotiations for modifying the Oath of Supremacy lessoned general interest in the whole debate.

'Extremist' was the epithet applied to Sir John by his adversaries, but his integrity and faith cannot be doubted. It is reflected in the elegant tribute which Joseph Berington composed in Latin to be inscribed on his friend's memorial in Buckland church.[2]

## Sir George Throckmorton, 6th baronet (1754–1826)

Coming into the title at his brother's death in 1819, Sir George preferred to live at Weston Underwood together with Lady Catherine, a Stapleton before her marriage. George was a semi-permanent invalid and suffered from gout. Among the books in the Priest's House at Harvington are a number of spiritual treatises with the baronet's signature inside their covers, which suggests that the invalid may have drawn some comfort from reading them during the long and tedious hours spent at home. Although living at some distance from Harvington, Sir George was aware of its spiritual needs and built St Mary's Church, which was opened a year before his death.

### Sir Charles Throckmorton, 7th baronet (1757–1840)

Demolished Weston, allowing Coughton Court to regain its prominence as the principal seat, although Sir Charles was a bachelor. With an interesting and unusual background, that of trained physician, a philanthropist and a natural historian, Sir Charles proved to be a popular lord among his tenants. The priests at Harvington also had good reason to be grateful to him for providing them in 1838 with considerably better accommodation than the Hall could offer.

### Sir Robert George Throckmorton, 8th baronet (1800–1862)

Married Elizabeth Acton, daughter of Sir John Acton of Aldenham, Shropshire. Sir Robert was Deputy Lieutenant of Berkshire in 1831, and was the first Catholic MP to take the Oath of Allegiance and sit in the House of Commons. His predecessor, Charles, had already moved some of Harvington Hall's best features to Coughton, and in 1855 his nephew, Sir Robert George, now took rather more, intending to demolish the building.

### Sir William Throckmorton, 9th baronet (1838–1919)

A bachelor, William's consuming interest was horses. He was a member of the Jockey Club and the National Hunt Committee. From the 1870s the baronet found his income diminished by both the agricultural depression and by his expensive hobby of racing. Buckland was sold in 1909 and soon the Throckmorton estates elsewhere, leaving Coughton to become the regular residence. The Great Staircase was taken from Harvington to Coughton and the Hall left to fall into complete ruin.

In 1921 Sir Richard Throckmorton, William's brother and 10th baronet, put both the Hall and the Hall Farm up for sale. The properties seem to have failed to reach their reserve, but in 1923 Mrs Ryan Ferris of King's Norton purchased the Hall, the church and the Priest's house, presenting them to the Archdiocese of Birmingham.

[1] Michael Hodgetts, 'The Throckmortons of Harvington 1696–1923', *Recusant History*, May 2002.
See also Vincent Hemingway, *Coughton Court and the Throckmortons*, Jarrold, 1993 and 1997.
[2] Kirk, Biog. p. 234.

# 8

# THE PEOPLE OF THE PARISH

## RECUSANTS IN CHADDESLEY CORBETT 1593–1594[1]

Recusant Roll 2 1593–1594 contains the following entries:
Humphrey Pakington, gent; recusant.
Ann, wife of William Mowsill.
George Bache, husb'. (husbandman)

The entry for Humphrey Pakington indicates that owing to the Act of 1586, in addition to the liability of having all his goods confiscated, he suffered the sequestration of two-thirds of his estates for failing to pay the fine for non attendance at the Anglican services. The estates included land in Shropshire and Worcestershire, including the manor house of Harvington, all of which were leased by the Lord Chancellor to William Sebright, a lawyer friend of Humphrey's and a native of Wolverley near Kidderminster. Sebright's lease terminated in February 1601–02, but other lessees followed until Pakington was finally released of all further liabilities to the State in 1607.

[1] C.R.S. vol. 57

## RECUSANTS IN CHADDESLEY CORBETT 1637–1767[1]

The following Catholics of the Harvington Mission were 'presented' to the authorities by the parish constables for non-attendance at the Anglican services in St. Cassian's or for recusancy. In Worcestershire from 1591 to 1643 there were approximately twenty-four persons indicted for recusancy but hundreds of presentments by the constables. Under the statute III Jac.I.cap.4 sec.3 parliament required churchwardens and constables in every town and parish to present the monthly absence of 'all manner of Popish recusants living there,' their children from the age of nine upwards, also the names of their servants, at the General of Quarter Sessions of the shire. These presentments were then recorded by the town clerk or his deputy. It seems however that a presentment under this statute did not of itself involve the recusant in any penalty, though failure to present had penal consequences for the defaulting constable.

Mary Bache, Widow            1637        Chadgsley Corbett
Presentment by John Hunt and Nicholas Rindon,
Chadgsley Corbett constables.

Mary Hunt, Widow            1637        Chadgsley Corbett
Presentment by John Hunt and Nicholas Rindon,
Chadgsley Corbett constables.

Elizabeth Jourdan            1637        Chadsley Corbett
Presentment by John Hunt and Nicholas Rindon,
Chadsley Corbett constables

Elizabeth Layte            1637        Chadsgley Corbett
Presentment by John Hunt and Nicholas Rindon,
Chadgsley Corbett constables.

Mrs Monk                1637        Chadgsley Corbett
Wife of Gregory
Presented by the constable.

Anthony Monk                19th April 1642
                        Chadgsley Corbett
Margaret Monk                19th April 1642
Wife of Anthony            Chadgsley Corbett

Mrs Parnell, Widow            1637        Chagsley Corbett
Presentment by John Hunt and Nicholas Rindon,
constables for recusancy.

Richard Layte                    1637        Chadgsley Corbett
Presentment by John Hunt and Nicholas Rindon
for recusancy.

## Churchwardens' Presentments

1674 'We present Humphrey Potter and Margaret, his wife, for not coming to our parish service and to sermon. We P'sent that a certain child of Benjamin Potter is un-baptized. We have none excommunicated that we know of. Nor do we know of any conventicles of non-conformist Quakers in our parish. But there are severall in our parish reputed Papists, which come not to church.'
William Leight)<br>Abram Blackway) Ch.W.

1682 'We humbly submit and say divers whom we remember not to have seen at church at time of Divine Service, pass under the notion of Popish Recusants and wee are informed are punished by the penall Lawes made and inflicted therefor, as Dame Mary Yate and some of her servants, as George Burford, Richard Bayliss, and some others whose names we certaynly know not. Others that are reputed Papists we remember not to have seene at church, but very poore: one Widdow Brooks, and Widdow Boorne, the wife of John Power, and some few others, whose names we know not certaynly. As for other Dissenters, there are some few who frequent not their parish church.'
Hen. Aston)<br>Tho.s James) Ch. W

1664 'We have no schizmatics or papists to our knowledge convicted, though we have families or papists in ye parish.'

1676 'Inhabitants of our parish that should be communicants are 447.

Popish Recusants, or supposed to be so, (of 16 years and upwards) are 28.

Other Dissenters who obstinately refuse to come to Church are 5.'
William Broughton.   Vicar<br>Edw. Morgan) Ch. Wardens<br>Gilbert Kimberley)

1679 'We think there are none in our parish that openly seduce people or entice them to separation, if that be meant by hereticks and schismatics, but we have some that hold not communion with us at the church, reputed to be papists; but of those 12 or more on the parish are reclaimed. There remains the Lady Yate and her servants, George Burford, Richard Bayleys, Robert Matthews, Matthias Giles, Elizabeth Reynolds, Mary Monk, and Jon. Bath, and some still persist in their opinion, we suppose for they communicate not with us.'

(Unsigned)

1674 'We doe not well understand the term of hereticks or Schismaticks, or who may call such, nor as we know are any Papists or any other sort, convict by law, or who may be said to refuse communion with the Church of England, or to profess another religion upon our certain knowledge, we cannot tell. But we answer that these persons of our parish doe not come to church: Dame Mary Yate and her family, John Cherrington, George Burford, Richard Bayleys, Robert Matthews, Matthias Giles, Margaret – (her surname we know not), Elizabeth Reynolds, Katherine Stafford and his wife, Stephen Chandler and his wife, Ann Reynolds, widow, Richard Reynolds, John Gurmell, Anthony Monk, William Raybold, Jane, the wife of ffrancis Scott, William Brook, Gervase Burford and Ann his wife, John Bayleys Junr., Isabel, the wife of Thomas Wilkes, Mary, the wife of John Power, Humphrey Potter and Margaret, his wife.'

William Broughton, Vicar
John Best) Ch. W.
Henry Raybould)

1682 'Ye parishioners for ye most part come duly to Church on the Lord's Days, but very few come on any other holy days. Most of the p'ishioners communicate at Easter, excepting them that pass for Papists.'

Joseph Smith
William Mole.Ch.W

1682 'Wee have not any that are reputed Hereticks or Schismaticks, nor any convicted Papists known, and Baptists, nor any that refuse to have their children Baptized.'

> Thomas Hooman. Min.
> Edmund Hornblower.
> Sidesman

1684 'We do not know of any that revile or rayle against the Church of England, or that refuse communion with it, except Dame Mary Yate, and some of her dependents, which are not now resident in the P'ish.'

> William Nock)
> John Kiteley) Ch. W.

1706 'The names of the Popish Recusants, householders, children, servants and sojourners as far as I can come to then knowledge of them, in the parish of Chaddesley Corbett, in the Diocese of Worcester, above 13 years of age: Joseph Green (Bailiff to Sir Robert Throckmorton, Lord of the Manor), and Elizabeth his wife; ffrances Drew his sister, Mrs. Helen Barrett, amd Mrs. Mary Spencer, sojourners;
John Litham, Ralph Guest, Henry Bagott, John Cotterell, Henry Holl, Charles Jones and John Barnbrook, Margaret Litham, Mary Hawkes, Mary Litham, Elizabeth Guest, Margaret Parker, Elizabeth Osburn, Mary Jones, Sarah Jones, and one maidservant more, whose name I have not information of.
Gervase Burnford, John Burnford and Clare, his wife, John Bayleys, Mrs. Cherrington (Widow), Ann Cherrington her daughter, Lucy Bache, Elizabeth Holden, Philip Barnbrook, Joice Barnbrook, Elizabeth Stowton, Susanna Stowton and Elizabeth Stowton, her daughter. Richard Bayleys, Elizabeth Bayleys his wife, Will Stafford, Magdalen Stafford his wife, Winifred Stafford their daughter, Thomas Russell, Ann Harper, John Pigeon, Ralph Raybould, ffrancis Bayleys, Joan, his wife, Alice Heath, Catherine harris, Emmanuel Laight, Jane Laight his daughter, John Bourn, John Gurmell, Thomas Litham and Margery his wife, Elizabeth Reynolds, Elizabeth Lamb, Edward Parker, Martha Fownes, IsabeyWilkes, Elizabeth Hubble, Joseph Sherry, Winifred his wife,

Elizabeth Bournford, Ann Bourn, widow, Ann Bourn her daughter,

Elizabeth Hashold.
I doe not understand that any of the parish come to church who abstain from the Sacrament out of affection for Popery.
Written and subscribed by me.'     William Broughton
                                    Vicar of Chaddesley Corbett

'There have been no levye madde of twelve pence a Sunday from such as have been absent from Church. I do believe there are non of the parishioners do designedly come late to Church, but being many live far from the Church sometimes it happens that they are mistaken in the time when they cannot heare no Bells.'
                              William Broughton. Vicar.

1714 'We present for not coming to Church the persons underwritten:
Mr. Joseph Green, Mr. Thomas Drew, Mr. John Allen, John Gurmell, John Litham, Thomas Lytham, John Bourne, William Power, Ralph Guest, Edw. Parker, Gervase Burford, John Burford, John bayliss, Richard Bayliss, ffran. halford, John Pigeon, John halford, Thos. Bache, Wm. Holden, Wm. Halford, Henry Payton, Eliz. Rose.'

John Broad)
Wm. Longmore) Ch. W

1767 'We present that a donation of twenty four pounds P.Ann. left by Lady Yates for the apprenticing of two children first to Papists, and in case there should be no Papists, to Protestant children, has been applied by Sr. Robt. Throckmorton, as Lord of the manner, in whom the application is vested, in the placing out the Children of Papists.'

William Aingworth
John Bate) Ch.W

[1] The above entries have been abstracted from R. Halstead, *Worcester Recusant*, no. 2, Dec. 1962, also from L. Lascelles and E. Guise-Berrow, *Worcester Recusant*, no. 6, Dec. 1965, no. 7, June 1966, also reference has been made to an article on Presentments by R. Halstead in *Worcester Recusant*, no. 3, July 1964. The list of Harvington's Catholics could of course be extended by the addition of recusants from the surrounding countryside and nearby towns, although with less certainty than those known to be living in the adjacent village.

## THE 1767 LIST OF CATHOLICS IN CHADDESLEY CORBETT PARISH

The list given below was drawn up in compliance with the *Returns of Papists* made throughout the country by the Anglican bishops to the House of Lords in 1767. The Diocese of Worcester made no less than 152 nil returns, so we are fortunate in having the Chaddesley Corbett information. The listing is interesting in that whole families are included along with ages, occupations and length of residence.

A comparison with the 1752 Baptism Register of Harvington reveals that the majority of those mentioned also occur in the Register and would have formed, together with other Catholics from beyond the Chaddesley boundaries, the worshipping community at Harvington. Due allowance being made for the lapsed, their names are given below rearranged in alphabetical order.

An account of all Papists and reputed Papists in the Parish of Chaddesley Corbett in the County and Diocese of Worcester taken this fifteenth day of August 1767.

        Vicar Thomas Bradley
        Churchwardens:-
John Bate and William

| Name | Age | Occupation | Residence |
|---|---|---|---|
| Catherine Baggot | 76 | | 55 Years |
| Randle Bagnal | 60 | Farmer | 26 Years |
| Jane, his wife | 59 | | 26 Years |
| Randle, his son | 27 | Farmer | 26 Years |
| Elizabeth, his daughter | 22 | | |
| Catherine Bayliss | 47 | | |
| Teresa Tracy(sic), her daughter | 16 | | |
| Joseph, her son | 14 | Mason of Harvington | |
| Catherine, her daughter | 12 | | |
| Anne, her daughter | 10 | | |
| Mary, her daughter | 8 | | |
| William Bradley | 16 | Locksmith | |
| John Bridgins | 20 | Servant | 14 Years |
| Thomas Bridgins | 70 | Flax Dresser | 15 Years |
| John Burford | 54 | Labourer | |
| Paul Butcher | 15 | Carpenter | 6 months |

| Name | Age | Occupation | Residence |
|------|-----|------------|-----------|
| William Crump | 15 | Servant of Bourne's Green | |
| Winifred Davies | 49 | Mantua maker | |
| Mary Dower | 55 | Widow, Pauper | 20 Years |
| Edward Edmunds | 14 | Servant | 6 months |
| Mary Farril | 59 | Widow | |
| Mary Foxall | 39 | Chaddesley | 18 Years |
| Sarah, her daughter | 17 | | |
| Ann, her daughter | 15 | | |
| Mary, her daughter | 7 | | |
| Joseph, her son | 5 | | |
| William, her son | 3 | | |
| Sarah Foxall | 18 | Servant | |
| Elizabeth Hall | 19 | Mantua maker | |
| John Hall | 54 | Wheelwright | 26 Years |
| Margaret, his wife | 56 | | |
| Elizabeth, their daughter | 25 | | |
| Ann, her daughter | 13 | | |
| Sarah, their daughter | 16 | | |
| William Instan | 20 | Labourer Chaddesley 2 Years | |
| Edward Johnson | 36 | Cordwainer in Harvington 12 Years | |
| Elizabeth, his wife | 35 | | |
| Charles, his son | 9 | | |
| Lydia Johnson | 75 | Widow | |
| Ann Johnson | 4 | | |
| William Johnson | 40 | Blacksmith | |
| Elizabeth, his wife | 36 | | |
| John, son of Wm & E. Jn. | 15 | | |
| William, their son | 13 | | |
| Mary, their daughter | 5 | | |
| Stephen Knight | 38 | Cooper | 13 Years |
| Ann Low | 30 | Servant | 20 Years |
| Dorothy Mason | 28 | Servant | 2 Years |
| Philip Pardoe | 46 | Cooper in Chaddesley | |
| John Pardoe, his son | 20 | Cooper | |
| Letitia, his daughter | 19 | | |
| Eleanor, his daughter | 18 | | |
| Elizabeth, his daughter | 16 | | |

| Name | Age | Occupation | Residence |
|---|---|---|---|
| Clare, his daughter | 13 | | |
| William Pardoe | 50 | Butcher, Chaddesley | |
| Nancy, his daughter | 20 | | turned |
| | | | about 3 years |
| Hannah, his daughter | 15 | | |
| Thomas, his son | 14 | Butcher, Harvington? | |
| Jane, his daughter | 12 | | |
| Charles Pardoe | 14 | Butcher | |
| Eleanor Pardoe | 12 | | |
| Thomas Pardoe | 11 | | |
| Edward Parker | 60 | Farmer | |
| Ann, his wife | 60 | | 30 Years |
| James Parker | 36 | Farmer, Bluntington Green | |
| Lucy, his wife | 30 | | 5 Years |
| Mary, his daughter | 3 | | |
| Ann, his daughter | 2 | | |
| John (Instan) his son | 12 | Chaddesley | 1 Year |
| George Parkes | 16 | Servant in | |
| | | Chaddesley | 6 months |
| Mary Penn | 50 | | 6 months |
| Mary Pointer | 51 | Mantua maker | |
| J. Roe Rowe? | 26 | Labourer of | |
| | | Winterfold | 1 Year |
| Elizabeth Rose | 63 | | 50 years |
| Ann Rea | 20 | Servant from Clent | |
| | | Harvington? | 18 months |
| Ann Silvester | 70 | | 19 Years |
| Elizabeth Silvester, Junr. | 30 | | |
| Elizabeth Silvester | 64 | Farmer | 40 Years |
| Thomas, her son | 36 | Farmer | |
| Jane, his wife | 34 | | 8 Years |
| Ann Stafford | 11 | from | 9 months |
| | | Belbroughton? | |
| Ann Styler | 20 | Servant to | |
| | | James Parker | 2 Years |
| William Thornhill | 64 | Labourer | 26 Years |
| Elizabeth Wall | 80 | Widow | |
| Arthur Vaughan | 40 | the Reputed Priest 11 Years | |

## WORCESTERSHIRE OATH TAKERS 1791–3[1]

The following between 1791 and 1793 took the oath of allegiance prescribed in the Catholic Relief Act of 1791. They are found in the Quarter Sessions records at Worcester Records Office, County Hall, Worcester. 118/6/6

**Translation Sessions, only 1791**
- f.27v  Mary Parker of Chaddesley Corbett, spinster
- f.27  Ann Parker of Chaddesley Corbett, spinster
- f.28  The mark of Arthur Vaughan of Chaddesley Corbett (minister in margins)
  Thomas Pardoe of Chaddesley Corbett, butcher
  James Mackrell of Grafton Manor, gentleman
  Edward Russell of Harvington, blacksmith
  John Parker of Chaddesley Corbett, husbandman

[1] Rhoda Murray, *Midland Catholic History*, no. 6, 1998.

## PAST PARISHIONERS 19TH–20TH CENTURY

The following names represent a tiny handful of all those who have been associated with the mission and parish of St Mary's, Harvington since the opening years of the nineteenth century. They are almost all buried in the churchyard, whereas those who died before the building of our church (including the priests) will have been buried for the most part in St Cassian's, Chaddesley Corbett. The chapel of St Nicholas in the village church remained in Catholic hands until 1864 when Sir Robert Throckmorton relinquished the ownership. Unfortunately the vault beneath, containing the remains of the Pakingtons and the early priests, was partially filled in with rubble when the church was restored around this time.

ARBUTHNOTT The Arbuthnotts arrived in the parish along with their school after the end of the Second World War. Hugh Arbuthnott founded, in 1925, Penryn School in Edgbaston as a Catholic Preparatory for boys, eventually transferring it to Winterfold House, Chaddesley Corbett, an attractive eighteenth-century mansion set in beautiful grounds overlooking the surrounding countryside and the Malvern Hills.

Harvington parishioners of the early 1900s.

Hugh Forbes Arbuthnott, a good traditional Catholic, came from a family that had provided no less than three priests for the church. The noted translator of the Bible, writer, hymnologist and eminent preacher, Ronald Arbuthnott Knox, was also a relation. Hugh Arbuthnott married Janet Marshall, the daughter of Vice-Admiral Herbert Marshall of Gayton Hall, Herefordshire, and a fervent convert to Catholicism. In addition to bringing up a family of eight children, Mrs Arbuthnott helped in the school, preparing the younger boys for their First Communion. With her help Fr Crichton, Harvington's priest in the 1950s, was able to form a choir made up of villagers and boys from Winterfold. The school's pupils also provided servers for the Mass as well as filling up half the church every Sunday.

Janet Arbuthnott was organist at St Mary's from 1949 to 1989 and something of an amateur; she once humbly asked the choir how the music could be improved and was unkindly told: 'by retiring the organist!' Nevertheless she will long be remembered as a co-founder, with Fr Geoffrey Tucker, of the Harvington Festival. This annual and largely musical event, is said to have been successful in spite of a sort of love-hate relationship between its promoters. In many ways, then, Janet Arbuthnott was a great worker for the parish. She and her husband, who was a Knight of Malta, are buried together in St Mary's. The church organ was renovated many years ago in Janet's memory, and a carved and gilded crucifix by Philip Lindsey Clarke above the baptismal font was donated by Hugh Arbuthnott.

Winterfold School no longer takes boarders and is now co-educational. It still continues to provide Catholic religious teaching and the parish priest of Harvington celebrates a weekly Mass there. A number of pupils, of course, are still involved in the parish, but Winterfold is now open to those of other faiths or none. How long it can retain its Catholic ethos remains to be seen.

BAGNALL Randle Bagnall, Jane his wife, Randle his son and Elizabeth his daughter are all listed as 'papists' living in the parish of Chaddesley Corbett in 1767. A Randle Bagnall is listed in the Directories of 1820 and 1840. He married Martha Hooper of Ludlow in 1799 at St Cassian's. Martha died in March 1839 and is buried in St Mary's churchyard. In November of the same year Randle married Elizabeth Parkes of a local Catholic family, but died in May 1840 aged seventy-two and was buried in St Mary's. His lease was taken over by the Mackrell family. The Bagnalls were farmers, leased land from the Throckmortons and lived in rooms at the Hall.

BAYLEY Helen Bayley was housekeeper to Rev P. Roskell. She had an unmarried sister who also helped at the priest's house for some time.

BAYLIS The Baylis family appears constantly in the records of Chaddesley Corbett. The earliest reference occurs in the Court Roll of 1409. At the Reformation and later a number of them remained Catholics and a Richard Baylis and his wife were among the trusted servants of Lady Mary Yate at the Hall. A branch of the family lived at Woodrow near Harvington and are mentioned in the registers of the Georgian Chapel and St Mary's. In 1816 Teresa Baylis married Thomas Emery, a Protestant, but the children were baptised Catholics. In the 1830s Thomas Baylis converted a smithy at Chaddesley into the Fox Inn and his grandson, Gregory, was steward to the Throckmortons.

BROOKS Mary Brooks was housekeeper to Rev J Marsden in 1816.

BROWNLOW Mary Ascough was born in Swinethorpe, Lincolnshire and was baptised 15 April 1759. She married Thomas Brownlow of Harby, Nottinghamshire in 1794. John, their only son, was born the following year and came to Harvington as priest in 1824. Thomas Brownlow died 4 October 1825, having become a Catholic two years previously; Mary his widow then seventy, moved to Harvington in 1829 to look after her son. In one of his many poems, Brownlow spoke lovingly of his mother and of his sorrow at her death:

> *My dear Mother liv'd and died like a Saint.*
> *Nature forc'd me to weep, and ever mourn and lament.*
> *Ah! how could I? Why should I? for whither she's gone,*
> *But to join the bless'd angels surrounding the throne of th'all*
> *beauteous, all – glorious,*
> *eternal Three – One.*

She died at 'The Chapel House', as it was then called, on 13 October 1852 aged nearly ninety-four. She and her son are buried side by side in St Mary's, but her tombstone has deteriorated.

CAMPBELL Bernard Campbell, originally from Cheltenham, came to live in Blakedown. He was a staunch Catholic and a member of the parish for twenty-three years. Bernard was married to Barbara for fifty-six years and had three sons. Called up at the outbreak of the

Second World War, he enlisted in the RAOC and was a Dunkirk veteran. On 4 June 1940 he was among some 338,226 men of the British and Allied Forces who were evacuated from this Channel port to safety. 800 civilian 'little ships' and 222 naval vessels took part in an operation which Churchill described as 'a miracle of deliverance'. Bernard departed from the beaches of Dunkirk, under fire, on a pleasure steamer.

After the war he started his own business in the motor trade, which he built up and managed until his retirement at the age of seventy. He died in 2001.

CHARE A Catholic family living at The Pound, Bluntington from at least 1860 until the beginning of the twentieth century, Robert Chare is listed as schoolmaster in Casseys 1860 *Directory*, but in the 1871 census his widow Elizabeth is described as a 'retired farmer'. In fact the Chares were bailiffs to the Throckmorton estate. Their daughter Catherine Chare was a teacher and a great supporter of St Mary's where the family graves are. By 1904 she was living in part of the Hall. The large carved oak chair for the priest was presented by Miss Christina Chare of Harvington Hall on 28 October 1907. Miss Christina and Miss Bessie Chare were 'poor relations' of the Throckmortons and *c*.1896 lived in the north tower of the Hall.

CLARKE Richard Clarke was the blacksmith at Harvington. According to the 1881 census he and Elizabeth, his wife, together with their six children, lived in the Hall. Brownlow: 'Clarke and wife seldom at chapel'.

CORBETT John Corbett of Harvington was a blacksmith. He died in 1843.

CUMMIN Bridget M. Cummin was housekeeper to Fr Wilson and lived at the Hall, according to the 1881 census. She came from Co. Tipperary in Ireland.

DAVIDSON The Davidson and Fletcher ledger tombstones outside the church door are unusual for their size and artistic engravings. Both were gentlemen farmers' families from Wollaston near Stourbridge and related. An aunt was an accomplished artist who executed the designs for the tombstones.

The Drinkwater family.

The Mearse, home of the Drinkwaters.

DRINKWATER The Drinkwaters are commemorated by several tombstones in St Mary's churchyard. Thomas George Drinkwater, known as George, was born at Beausale House near Kenilworth, Warwickshire in 1848 and educated at Ratcliffe, the Rosminian college in Leicestershire. As a young man he assisted his father, John, in running the farm at Beausale until the agricultural depression of the 1870s led to the sale of the estate. As a result George moved to Brierley Hill, Staffordshire, where he set up as a draper and presently married Alice, the eldest daughter of William Corvesor, grocer of Dudley. George and Alice had three sons and four daughters and in a time built up a flourishing business with shops in Stourbridge and Kidderminster. With his improved financial situation George began to reconsider a return to farming, and in 1894 he purchased The Mearse Farm near Harvington with its 170 acres from Sir William Throckmorton. This was followed a few years later by the further purchase of some cottages and land in Harvington itself. Here he built a house originally called 'West View' but soon renamed 'Beausale'. Some of this property was rented to a family named Corbett, but in 1903, one of George's sisters, Agnes, moved in. Agnes had lived abroad for many years, being governess to the Princesses Aldobrandini and living with that family in Rome and Frascati. Soon after her arrival, another unmarried sister, Kate, came to live with her, and it is said that the young people of the parish used to go to them to be fitted out with their hats, an important and regular part of dress in those days.

In 1899 George, who was always making improvements to The Mearse, built a lodge at the end of the drive and the family, which had divided their time between Brierley Hill and their farm near Harvington, settled permanently in Worcestershire. However, no sooner had they made the final move than tragedy struck. The second daughter, Katie, had been at school at the English Convent in Paris (where two of George's sisters were nuns) and, aged sixteen and already ill, came home and died on 24 August that year. She was the first of the family to be buried at Harvington.

In 1902 George decided to lease the Mearse farm and William Benedict Oakley (qv) took on the tenancy and lived at the lodge until his sudden death some six years later. George Drinkwater himself died at The Mearse in 1916, to be followed many years later by Alice. Their graves are by the churchyard wall in St Mary's. George's sisters remained at Beausale cottage in the village until their deaths in the 1930s. Other members of the family buried here include George's brother, Julian, who had once farmed in Canada and then returned to live in Herefordshire, and George's sister, Mary Helen Clare, who married Felix Moore, George's onetime business partner in Brierley Hill. 'Baby Joseph' buried by the churchyard gate was the grandson of George Drinkwater, and Pearl Harper, the last of the family to be buried here, was Mary and Felix's granddaughter.

Finally, it is perhaps worth remembering that two of George Drinkwater's nephews were priests of the Birmingham archdiocese. They were sons of Francis James Drinkwater of Wednesbury: Fr John Drinkwater (1888–1963) and his better known brother Monsignor Canon Harold Drinkwater (1886–1982), who did so much work as a pioneer catechist after the First World War, founded *The Sower* magazine and was Diocesan Inspector of Schools.

DUGARD Albert Dugard became custodian of the Hall in 1933; he also took a job in 1939 with the RAF at Hartlebury, cycling back and forth. His wife, Etta, kept the house open on three afternoons a week, guiding visitors and supplementing her slender knowledge of its history with her fertile imagination.

ELWELL There were two branches of this family and members of both are buried in St Mary's. Elwell was a farmer in Churchill near Blakedown and married a Miss Hayward of Harvington. Their children walked four and a half miles to school at Harvington.

EMERY Thomas Emery, listed in the 1860 *Directory*, was an attorney supposed to have worked for the Harward family of Winterfold House, but according to the *Directory* he also had his own offices in Church Street, Kidderminster. He was born in Chaddesley in 1796, the son of John and Ann Emery. In 1817 he married Teresa Baylis, daughter of Joseph and Elizabeth Baylis and they lived in the main street in Chaddesley. A son, George, was born in 1824 and baptised at St Mary's. He died in 1826, the same year as his father, and both were buried in the village church. His widow continued to live in Chaddesley until at least 1841, sharing a cottage next to The Talbot with her sister Mary Baylis.

FERRIS In November 1923 Ellen Ferris purchased Harvington Hall at the cost of £1,100, saving this historic house for the Church. She also secured St Mary's and the Priest's House, presenting the whole complex to the Archdiocese of Birmingham. Before her marriage in her early thirties she ran a dressmaking business in Leicester which

The Elwell and Hayward families, *c*.1927.

enjoyed Royal Patronage. But around 1900 she moved to Kings
Norton, Birmingham, to help her brothers establish a huge housing
estate which they had worked very hard to build up, together with the
parish church and the local pub called the The Grant Arms. Ellen,
married to a doctor, was Miss Grant before her marriage. Their son,
Lord Harvington, added Grant to his surname Ferris in recognition of
all that his mother's side of the family had done to build up the family
fortune. He never knew his father, Dr Ferris, an alcoholic, whom
Ellen would not tolerate in the house. Nevertheless, Ferris was highly
esteemed among several of his patients around Newcastle.

Ellen Ferris had a very strong devotion to the English martyrs,
especially St John Wall, and collected their relics. She was regarded
as an eccentric on account of the very large hats she wore to church
on Sundays which, since she always sat in the front row, blocked
people's view of the altar. Perhaps the hats expressed her personality,
since she lived life to the full and did everything with great enthusi-
asm. She died in 1955.

FORD Agnes Ford, born 1902, was the daughter of Martin Ford of Aston, Deritend, a butcher journeyman. Soon after birth she was left on Father Roskell's doorstep and was brought up by his housekeepers, the Misses Bayley. Philip Roskell generously paid for Agnes to be educated by the nuns at the convent in Southam. Despite her unfortunate beginning, Agnes grew to be a happy child and later married Stephen Morris of Southam in St Mary's, Harvington.

The couple lived for a short while at the Hall and Agnes's first child, Philip, named after Father Roskell, was born in the room next to Dr Dodd's library, as was a second child, Patricia. Agnes Ford sadly died in childbirth in 1936, having by then moved to Knowle.

Stephen Morris who is mentioned as thurifer at the centenary Mass at St Mary's in 1925, married again and went to live in Wales. His Requiem Mass, however, was celebrated at Harvington in 1990 and he was buried in Birmingham with his first wife. Other members of the Ford family are buried in Harvington.

FOXALL The Foxalls, mentioned as 'papists' in 1767 still occur in the Harvington register in 1837.

GRANT Denis and Betty Grant came to live in Kidderminster in 1937. Denis became manager of the Trustee Savings Bank. They had five children: Denise, Robert (Bob), Clive, Andrew and Luke. They all became regular parishioners in the mid-1950s and the boys were altar servers. Betty taught at Winterfold in 1948 and 1949 and subsequently at Birchen Coppice Primary School for several years. She died in 1970. Denis was sidesman at the 8.30 Mass for many years until involved in a car accident when he went to live with his son, Andrew.

In 1975 Denis married Elizabeth Carey. She died in 1987 and is buried in St Mary's. Clive was a passenger in a car accident on Stone Hill and never fully recovered. He died in 1980. Denis died in 1990. Robert married Shirley Maguire in 1962. At that time the Maguires were curators at the Hall. The Grants continued their long association with the Hall. The family grave is just outside the church door and adjacent to the Maguire family grave.

GRIFFIN George Griffin, the son of Mr and Mrs H. Griffin of Purshall Green, Rushock, was a Private 1st/7th Battalion Royal Warwickshire regiment, who died 5 May 1919 aged twenty-two. His grave is marked by a recent military gravestone.

The Hailes family of the Hall Farm with Fr Clement Harris.

HAILES This old Catholic family occupied the Hall Farm in late Victorian times and into the twentieth century. Three generations are buried in St Mary's. Edward Hailes who died in 1896, aged eighty-three, came from Neen Sollars, near Cleobury Mortimer.[1] An Edward Hailes is noted in 1780 as a recusant and servant to Mr Thomas Wall of that place, and a rough pedigree in a family Bible mentions an Edward who was born in 1763. This Edward had a sister Frances Teresa, who was a professed lay sister in the convent of Augustinian canonesses in Paris and who died in 1835, aged seventy-six, having been a religious for over fifty years. There was also a second nun, Justina Ann Hailes who died at the same convent in 1829.[2] Canon Barry in his *Memoirs and Opinions* quoted on p. 60 speaks of the long association of the family with the Dames Anglaises in the Rue Picpus, and that two of its members in succession ruled the convent for 'no less than forty years'. He also says that the second Mother Superior was still living when he visited Paris in 1885. This does not tie in with the foregoing family documentation.

Edward Hailes came to the Hall Farm from Shropshire to farm 275

Edward Hailes senior, with the stool discovered by his grandson in the
Library 'hide' at Harvington Hall, 1894.

acres of Sir William Throckmorton's land, employed seven labourers
and a boy. As well as the family there were also four servants, so
perhaps the seventeenth-century farmhouse was enlarged at this time.
Edward Mary Hailes married Anne Mary Spink; Mrs Hailes was a
generous benefactor and gave a monstrance and chalice to the church.
Edward died at the early age of fifty-five in 1912.

Finally, Edward Thomas Hailes, his son, was for sometime parish
council clerk and assistant overseer for Chaddesley Corbett. For many
years he was a playing member of the local cricket team until he lost
a leg in the First World War during which he served in the Middlesex Regiment. Returning to civilian life he resumed his previous occupation as a solicitor in Worcester until his retirement. Like his parents
and grandparents, he was a regular and devout parishioner of St
Mary's, and was presented with a large Latin missal by Fr Philip
Roskell, suitably inscribed and recording Edward's faithful service
over nine years as an altar server.

At his father's death Edward went to live with his mother near

Droitwich. During the Second World War, despite his disablement, he took a lively interest and active part in the local Home Guard. He died in 1955 and was buried in Harvington.

[1] Norman Mutton, 'Shrophire Recusants 1767 and 1780', *Worcestershire Recusant*, 26, Dec. 1975.
[2] Obituaries, *Laity's Directory*, C.R.S. vol.12, p. 211 and Hailes Pedigree, HPA.

HANBURY This family, in spite of the name, were Irish and from Limerick. They were woolcombers in Kidderminster. James Hanbury, who died aged nineteen in 1834, now has the oldest surviving tombstone in St Mary's.

HARRIS Maria Harris, 1825–1913, had been school teacher at Harvington after Mary Kellard. She lived in the Withdrawing Room at the Hall and died in 1913 at the age of eighty-eight. She was noted for her Victorian-style curls.

HARVINGTON Harvington was born Robert Grant-Ferris, the son of Robert Grant-Ferris, a doctor, and Ellen Ferris who gave Harvington Hall to the archdiocese. After being educated at Douai Abbey School he read law and was called to the Bar by Inner Temple, in 1937. Already interested in politics he was elected a Birmingham City councillor in 1933, and two years later unsuccessfully contested Wigan before eventually capturing St Pancras North at a by-election for the Conservative Party.

On the outbreak of war, having already joined the RAF Auxiliary Reserve (Warwick) he was promoted to wing commander. He served in Malta, the Middle East and Europe. His seat at St Pancras fell in the Labour landslide in 1945, and he unsuccessfully fought Wandsworth Central in 1950 and 1951 before winning Nantwich in 1955. This he held until 1974. From 1970 to 1974 he was Deputy Speaker of the House of Commons and brought to the Chair good humour combined with firmness. Without being pompous he could be a stickler for etiquette. He was the only Conservative MP to be both knighted and created a peer under Labour administrations.

He was also the only Conservative among twelve new peers announced by Harold Wilson in 1974. At Westminster he was one of that diminished class, long the backbone of the Conservative Party, the squirearchy, for whom politics was a duty rather than a career. The family estate was at Tetbury, Gloucestershire.

Grant-Ferris came from a leading English Catholic family, and was one of a number of Catholics on the Conservative benches. He was chamberlain to Pope Pius XII and Pope John XXIII, his wide experience providing a valuable link between the Conservative government and the Vatican. On retiring from the Commons in 1974, Harvington went to live in Jersey, paying only occasional visits to England to speak in the Lords. A noted breeder of pedigree sheep and one-time president of the National Sheep Breeders' Association, he suffered heavy losses when New Zealand and Australia banned imports from Britain because of scrapie. As a younger man Harvington had become an accomplished yachtsman, and was Honorary Admiral of the House of Commons Yacht Club. In the mid-1970s, Mrs Thatcher and husband joined Harvington aboard his yacht *Melita* for summer holidays; canals were another of his interests and the subject of his maiden speech in the Lords.

He was knighted in 1969 and sworn of the Privy Council in 1971. Harvington was deputy-chairman of the board of *The Tablet*, and patron of many Catholic organisations. In 1949 he was made Knight Grand Cross of Magistral Grace of the Sovereign Order of Malta (with Riband, 1985).

In the same order he was awarded the Grand Cross of Merit with Star (1953). In 1930 he married Florence Brennan De Vine, who predeceased him and is buried in Jersey. Lord Harvington, who died on 1 January 1997, is buried in St Mary's together with his mother.

HASKEW The origins of the Haskews or Ayscoughs are to be found in the far north of the country. But the Staffordshire branch appears to have moved *c.*1500 from Kelsey in Lincolnshire to Hopwas between Tamworth and Lichfield.[1] It was here that they are said to have acquired the prefix 'H', which they clung to as a distinguishing mark of their particular branch and their Catholicity; for there were Protestants of the name, not the least the sixteenth-century martyr, Anne Askew, who was burnt at Smithfield. The Staffordshire Haskews remained staunch adherents of the faith and made their farm, Hopwas House, available as a Mass centre. In 1810 James Haskew married Hannah Pipe of Pipe Hall, another Catholic Mass centre nearby. John Kirk, the priest who was due to become chaplain at Harvington, looked after these old missions for a short while, but the two congregations were united at Lichfield when Pipe Hall was sold in 1800 and Kirk moved into the city soon after. The former Catholic chapel with its graveyard still survives at Hopwas.

Matthew Haskew who was born in 1823 was a devout Wolverhampton Catholic and one of his children, Clement, was ordained
for the diocese in 1888 and served in several parishes, including
Bromsgrove, where he died. Another Haskew, Philip Alfred, born
in 1827, the tenth child of James and Hannah mentioned above, came
from Wiggington near Hopwas. Together with his wife, Mary Ann
(nee Bate) from Wolverhampton, he came to Harvington about 1865
to farm 138 acres of Throckmorton land. It is thought that Philip
was also caretaker at the Hall and that he discovered some of the
hides there. A daughter, Mary Helen or Ellen married Henry Brierley, licensee of The Dog in Harvington; they later emigrated to
Canada.

A beautifully bound Latin altar missal was presented to St Mary's
in memory of Philip Haskew after his death, by his wife and daughter. A seventeenth-century bench in the church also commemorates his
wife who died in 1904.

[1] Pedigree HPA.

HAYWARD Harry Hayward, father of the Rev Bernard Hayward,
had the village shop, which stood to the front of the present building.
He taught the Sunday School both from his shop and latterly from St
Mary's. A slightly odd sight, he was covered in thick blankets in all
weathers because of malaria, which he had contracted during the First
World War. When out and about he had an adapted bicycle with a tea
chest on the front in which he could transport two children.

HIGGINS T Dermott Higgins (1900–1986) was the only reader at
8.30 a.m. Mass for many years; he also acted as sidesman together
with Robert Hodgkinson until shortly before his death. His hobby was
carpentry and he made candlesticks and collection plates for the
church. Higgins, who lived at The Pound Cottage, Chaddesley
Corbett, took an active part in the social life of the village and the
annual Catholic Ball committee of Harvington Hall.

HIGLEY The Higleys came from Rushock and intermarried with
other long-established Harvington parishioners – the Elwells and the
Roberts. They are mentioned in the parish registers in 1890 and subsequently. Francis Higley with his six brothers and sisters lived at
Steppes Farm, Harvington Hall Lane, which in the late nineteenth
century was a working farm.

The Higley children attended the Harvington School and were packed off to St Mary's three times on Sundays. Jack Higley was in charge of the Post Office which formerly existed in Mustow Green.

HODGKINSON Henry Robert Hodgkinson (1872-1959) a solicitor from Droitwich, acquired the Hall Farm with its tenant in 1934, and, although not a farmer, he moved in there in 1947 when the tenant vacated the premises. From 1930-1951 he was secretary of the Hall Committee and gave or influenced nearly all the money raised for the continuance of the Halls' restoration. Much of its furniture was donated through him by the National Trust, and in 1940 and 1946 he gave covenants to the Trust restricting twenty-seven acres of land round the Hall to use for farming only. Hodgkinson moreover enlisted a few of his friends to help him with some of the heavy physical labour and restoration work on the Hall, thus saving expenditure the Committee could ill afford. Although an archaeologist and Fellow of of the Society of Antiquaries, he had not researched the history of the Hall, and his influence over the Committee led it to sink most of its funds into reprinting a very inaccurate series of articles by Christopher Hussey from *Country Life*. This was part of the problems that arose with the Hall management in 1954-1957. A further difficulty was Hodgkinson's autocratic disposition and his conviction that the future of the Hall could only be assured if his own position was made hereditary. By 1950 one of his sons was joint secretary with him, another was treasurer, and when it was pointed out that more women were needed on the Committee, he suggested that his wife would be suitable.

Hodgkinson is buried in the churchyard attached to St Catherine's Church, Droitwich, a splendid basilica-style building erected through the munificence of his father, Walter L Hodgkinson of Rashwood Court. As generous as ever, his son, R B Hodgkinson, added a chapel dedicated to St Richard in 1938.

ILSLEY Joseph Ilsley was schoolmaster at Harvington for more than forty years. He was married to Isabella Hall in 1837 and they had four children. Joseph, John, Mary and William. Joseph was the uncle of Archbishop Ilsley. Both Joseph and his wife are buried side by side in St Mary's.

KEEFE Charles and his wife Alice were curators at the Hall in the 1970s. Alice was a forthright character with an obsession for cleaning which earned her the name 'Mops'.

LEWIS William Lewis kept a shop in Mustow Green from at least 1862 until his death in 1873, after which the business was carried on by his wife until sometime after 1876. William Lewis was a Catholic and is buried in St Mary's.

MACKRELL The Mackrells were another Catholic family who lived and farmed at Harvington Hall Farm, leased from the Throckmortons. James Mackrell, listed as a gentleman in the 1820 *Directory*, came from Shifnal in Shropshire and married Elizabeth Silvester of Chaddesley Corbett in 1772, Randle Bagnall being a witness. He died in 1820 aged seventy-seven and was buried in Chaddesley. James, junior, listed in 1820 and 1840, was probably baptised in the Georgian Chapel at the Hall, and was buried in St Mary's in 1848. Apparently, he had been a great sportsman, so when he became too infirm for a day's shooting he amused himself by shooting rats in the barn.

MAGUIRE Angus Denys Maguire, known as Denys, was born in 1907 in Wimbledon, the only son of Angus and Frances Maguire (née Perks). He had one sister Joan, born in 1914. He was educated by the Jesuits at Wimbledon College, and was a contemporary of Hugh Arbuthnott. He married Joyce Kathleen Cole in 1934, who had been educated at the Ursuline Convent in Wimbledon. They were married in India.

Denys had been an analytical chemist before he joined the Indian Police Force and was based in Bihar (one of the poorest states of India). He was awarded the Indian Police Medal, presented to him by Lord Wavell in 1943 or thereabouts. There were three children – Shirley, Bridget and Michael. The girls were educated at the Loretto Convent in Darjeeling, Michael being too young to go to school in India. The family came back to England in 1945, and settled in Devon where his mother and sister were living, later moving to Wolverhampton where his mother's family came from. Denys went back to India and finally retired in 1947 with the rank of Senior District Superintendent. He then went to Egypt during the Suez crisis as a police liaison officer. As he was fluent in Hindi and other dialects, he was one of the few people allowed out of the Canal Zone and into the local bazaars to listen and gather information. He and Joyce moved to Harvington Hall from Oxley, Wolverhampton, as curators in 1957. The Hall at that time had no mains water or drainage. The water came via an electric pump from a well and had to be boiled. The sanitation, Elsans chemical toilets, had to emptied by the curators. The main hall was not heated, and as there were no lights in the upper part of the building, the Hall was shut as soon as it became too dark to see. The catering kitchen had been condemned so all food had to be cooked in the curator's side of the hall and brought over to the tea room. The curator's side of the hall was heated by a coal fire in the sitting room, a solid fuel cooker in the kitchen which heated the water, and electric fires in the bedrooms. The bathroom under the stairs, which had an outside door to the moat, was very cold. Mains water came to the Hall in 1959 and mains drainage in 1961. Denys Maguire died in 1962 and is buried in St Mary's, Harvington.

Bridget married Cedric Marshall. She died in 1972 and is buried in Scotland. Shirley married Bob Grant and Michael married Judith Preedy. After Denys died Joyce carried on running the Hall for a short while and subsequently became Matron at Winterfold, and in the summer holidays she worked at Butlins. She eventually went to live with Michael at Tardebigge. Joyce died in 1988 and is buried with her husband just outside the entrance to the church.

OAKLEY William Benedict Oakley was a farmer in Chaddesley in the early twentieth century. His family was united by marriage to the large Catholic family of the Collingwoods which provided many priests and nuns for the church. They were connected with Hull and Corby Glen, but a number of Oakleys settled around Chaddesley Corbett.

PARDOE Thomas Pardoe who was living in Chaddesley in 1791, was a butcher. The family remained Catholic and are mentioned in the Harvington register in 1858.

PARKER The Parkers were an old Catholic family in Purshall Green and farmers. James Parker, who died in 1849, was the last of a long line.

PARKES It was Ann Parkes, servant to James Mackrell, who was sacristan to the Georgian Chapel in Mr Marsden's time and discovered the penal days' chalices, vestment and book hidden inside the wooden altar. These would have been brought out but for the unfortunate fire which destroyed part of the chapel in 1823. Thomas Parkes, who died in 1872 aged seventy-nine, was her husband and lived at Hall Farm. His father, also Thomas, lived on the neighbouring estate at Grafton.

May Parkes was housekeeper to Rev J. Marsden in 1819.

PEDLEY Brigadier-General Stanhope Humphrey Pedley, CB OL, late Royal West Kent Regiment, bought 'Monks' at the corner of Woodrow and Harvington Road in 1921. He was first president in 1926 of the newly-formed Chaddesley and Stone and District Royal British Legion. He died in 1938. His wife, Mary Leonie Pedley, was a stalwart of the parish and great support to its priest. During the Second World War she assisted the war effort by her work for food preservation and canning. By 1940 she was living at Eastcote, Brockencote. She was much involved in the Women's Institute at county level and was chairman 1937–1954. She died in 1957. They are buried together close to the entrance to the church. A silver ciborium also perpetuates their memory.

RADCLIFFE The Radcliffes were originally an old Northumbrian gentry family who, like their neighbours the Charltons and Widdringtons, remained loyal to the Catholic faith. Their home at Dilston between Hexham and Newcastle, still remains together with its chapel, although the house is now a shell and the chapel given over to Anglican worship. During the political and religious turmoil of the 1590s the Radcliffes retired to the safety of the Lake District. Later James Radcliffe, Earl of Derwentwater, a leading Jacobite, was executed after the uprising of 1715.[1] Cyril William Joseph Radcliffe was the son of Bernard and Georgina Radcliffe.

His grandfather was Sir Joseph, 3rd baronet, married to Katherine Doughty Tichborne; the Radcliffes were also linked with other ancient Catholic families such as the de Traffords, Turvilles and Constable-Maxwells. Cyril was educated by the Jesuits at Stonyhurst as was his father, and eventually established Radcliffes Brewery in Kidderminster. He and his wife, Joan (known as 'Bobbie'), came to live at Norchard Grange, Hartlebury, around 1940. The brewery was later taken over by Butlers, although Cyril stayed on as a director. His young cousin, Sir Sebastian Radcliffe, Bt., was educated at Winterfold.

To his friends Cyril appeared as rather a private person and as someone put it – 'straight as a gun barrel'. Radcliffe became a Knight of Grace and Devotion in the Order of Malta, and made a point of attending weekday Mass. For many years, too, he was Chairman of the Bench in Stourport and a member of the management Committee of Harvington Hall from 1951 to 1955. His leisure activities included racing and shooting. His chauffeur, Reeves, regularly motored him to the Cheltenham Races, having first ensured that the boot was well

Pleremore, the home of the Trafford family.

stocked with an ample supply of liquid refreshment. Cyril Radcliffe died in 1981, his wife following him two years later. The tombstone is inscribed with the cross of the Knights of Malta.

[1] Kirk, Biog., pp. 194–6.

REDDIN James was one of a number of Irish woolcombers of Kidderminster to be buried in St Mary's in the early 1800s. He was also a blacksmith at his house in Mustow Green.

RUSSELL Another Harvington family from at least the eighteenth century. Edward Russell was the village blacksmith in the 1800s.

SPINK Charles Spink of Mustow Green had been at Sedgley Park and later became tutor to the Bavarian Arco-Vallei family. In Littlebury's *Directory* of 1876 he is described as 'Machinist' of Mustow Green and in 1886, as living at Muster (*sic*) Lodge. He died on Christmas Eve, 1885, aged sixty-nine and his widow, Anne, later commissioned the fine east window in St Mary's which features various saints and martyrs, including St Charles Borromeo, her husband's patron. A ciborium was given to the parish with the inscription: 'AMDG (*Ad majorem Dei gloriam*) *Ex dono Caroli Spink ora pro eo et familia ejus*'.

TRAFFORD The Traffords trace their lineage back to the thirteenth century with the principal family seat at Trafford Park, Lancashire. Sir Edmund Trafford, knighted in 1603, was thrice High Sheriff of the county; he was no friend of recusants, but Sir Cyril Trafford, a Puritan, was converted to the faith of his ancestors by Francis Downes, Catholic lord of Wardley Hall. Downes was thus instrumental in securing to the Church a family which has ever since been conspicuous for its fidelity and devotion – with the occasional exception. John Trafford of Crostan married Katherine, daughter and co-heir of Thomas Culcheth, Lancastershire, in 1688, thus bringing this property into the family. The Will of William John Francis Trafford (1828) says that he was 'late of Culcheth Hall in the county of Lancaster but now of Pleremore' in Chaddesley Corbett. William's brother was Thomas Joseph Trafford of Trafford Park. Thomas was created 1st baronet in 1841 and styled 'De Trafford' by royal licence. The change of style is reflected on the two memorials in St Mary's.

Along with the house and its contents in Chaddesley, William also bequeathed to his wife, Mary, his 'farming stock and instruments of husbandry whatsoever and all my other stock in the aforesaid things' – which indicates that he was a gentleman farmer. Other beneficiaries mentioned are his cousin, Charles Tempest of Houghton Hall, Yorkshire, and a friend Thomas Scarisbrick of Scarisbrick, near Ormskirk – both prominent Catholics.[1] William Trafford had two children, William and Jemima. According to his large memorial tablet in St Mary's, Harvington, he died in 1829 after a long illness bravely borne and aged only forty-seven.

A family vault was constructed in the church to take four burials, but probably only contains himself and his son Walter. Mary Trafford was a convert to Catholicism; after her husband's early death she married William Acton of Wolverton at St Mary's, 22 October 1833. They lived at Pleremore until the 1870s. Around this time Walter de Trafford and his wife Mary came to live at Pleremore House and had three children: Monica, Henrietta and Humphrey. An Irish governess was employed to look after them and there were also a couple of servants. Captain Trafford was a county magistrate and took a great interest in local affairs. He later retired to Malvern Link where he died in 1901, aged seventy-seven. He was buried in the Trafford vault back at Harvington.[2]

[1]   Will of William Trafford HPA.
[2]   Elizabeth Tangye, *The Families and Village of Chaddesley Corbett*.

WATTS Humphrey Ignatius Watts was born in 1879 in Edgbaston and was the second son of William Henry Watts and his wife Mildred, a daughter of John Hardman Powell. With this maternal link with the family of the celebrated Gothic Revival architect, A W Pugin, it was perhaps not surprising that Humphrey soon manifested a fascination with architecture. Tutored by the Jesuits at Stonyhurst along with his two brothers (one of whom, Philip, became a member of the Society), Humphrey went on to read architecture at Liverpool University, later becoming articled to Leonard Stokes. But on the death of his father in 1902 he was obliged to give up his career to become head and managing director of the family brass-rolling business in Birmingham. Architecture and art however remained his hobby throughout his life.

Tall with a slight stoop, a keen observant look and a quiet but sociable disposition, Humphrey met his perfect companion somewhat late in life. Ethel Maud Poulton, whom he married in 1935, was a former university lecturer in Birmingham and at Queen's College, Belfast; she was in addition a writer and musical composer. Humphrey too delighted in music and both of them were particularly interested in church music and its improvement. As the years went by Sion House, their home, reflected more and more the artistic tastes which they shared in common; and it radiated happiness.

The mansion had extensive and very lovely grounds stretching down to the hamlet of Hillpool. The present house dates from about 1800 and once belonged to Sir William Oldnall Russell, Chief Justice of Bengal who died in 1833. Humphrey and Ethel Watts probably moved there after their marriage, furnishing the rooms with artistic treasures, pictures, sculpture and the like, including a magnificent and ornamental grand piano on which Ethel played works by her favourite Romantic composers. It was the hope of this devout couple that one day they would build a little church in the grounds dedicated to St Thomas More, a man they much admired. Sadly, that was not to be.

Humphrey fell ill and his condition was soon diagnosed as cancer of the liver. When Fr Crichton, the parish priest, visited him he was edified to see a copy of the Greek New Testament lying on the patient's bed. After considerable suffering death came as a merciful release; he was in his seventieth year. Crichton noted that Humphrey Watts had a little of the oddity of his ancestor, Pugin; his speech was somewhat abrupt and he had certain prejudices. He was never, however, aggressive. That being said, when he was running the business his office staff and his servants remembered the real affection he had for them. His Catholic faith was both practical and genuine. After his death in 1949, Ethel and Fr Crichton agreed that a fitting memorial to Humphrey would be the insertion of the figure of St John Wall, the Harvington martyr, into the east window of the church and the panelling of the sanctuary walls – by then suffering from the effects of damp. The work was carried out by Cecil Parker, an organist and craftsman, who also fixed an appropriately worded memorial tablet in the sanctuary. Humphrey Watts is buried at Blackmore Park near Upton-upon-Severn. Ethel, who retired to Oxfordshire, died some thirty years later.

WEBSTER Veronica and Lionel Webster from Hagley lived at the Hall in the 1950s with Veronica as official curator. Both had been solicitors, but Lionel volunteered to join the RAF in which he became an officer. After leaving the Air Force he went on to teach at Oakham

The Watts family.

Sion House, home of the Watts family.

School. Both he and his wife had the reputation for being cultured people with an extensive knowledge of historical, antiquarian and artistic matters. Their stay at Harvington Hall turned out to be short since relations with the Management Committee quickly soured.

In February 1957 Veronica Webster was served with three months' notice to quit, and the Hall which closed early in May was reported by the local press to be 'virtually in a state of siege'. Mrs Webster was restrained from removing any goods of the Management Committee or from showing visitors round the Hall. An anonymous squib composed at the time in the style of a seventeenth-century ballard reflects the grievances of the Committee.

## A WORCESTERSHIRE LAMENT

(Attributed to Bl John Wall)

O woe is me! Ye woman still resides
Despite my Lord Archbishop's urgent call
That she forthwith quit my holy hides.

But she, efficient, bolted fast ye door
That none may entrance gain unto the Hall
Till such time as His Grace's Suit at law
Shall forcibly evict her – dogges and all.

Meantime her spouse (acquiring sudden fame)
In *Tablet, Herald, Universe* and *Poste*
Doth all he can to run down Mistress Yate
And of Endowment Funds unseemly boast;
Yea – e'en from open casement doth proclaim
To eager Pressmen gathered at ye gate
How sore aggrieved his wyffe is by the action
Committee book to end her ruthless thrust
Despite all bogus 'Friends' of Red Brick faction[1]
Whose impudence invokes ye Nat'nal Trust.

O Truth, come forth and end this sad disgrace
That doth besmirch our fair name far and wide.
O Law, be swift! Pursuivants, urge your pace
And chuck 'em out – their kant I can't abide!

---

[1]   A reference to Birmingham University graduates and undergraduates among the friends who had been critical of the Committee.

Fr Crichton, who had pleaded for a sympathetic understanding of the Websters' difficulties on the one side and for loyalty and cooperation on the other, was himself unfeelingly transferred to Pershore soon afterwards. Veronica, dying in 1992, is buried together with her daughter, Berenice, in St Mary's churchyard.

The tragic death of Berenice who died eight months after the Websters came to Harvington, undoubtedly cast a shadow over her parents' years at the Hall.

YATES Mary Yates, who came from Wolverhampton, was a house-keeper to Fr Brownlow in his retirement.

# 9

# THE HARVINGTON LIBRARY OF THE SECULAR CLERGY

In 1964 G. F. Pullen published an incomplete Catalogue of the books in the Recusant Library at Oscott College.[1] In that library the books originally housed at Harvington Hall form a significant number. They comprise works of controversy and devotion relating to the Church in England since the Reformation and are an important record of Catholic life throughout the Penal Days. The Harvington books are usually inscribed with the words *Bib[liotheca] Harv[ingtoniensis] Clae[ricorum] Saec[ularium]*, or *B.H.C.S.* The collection includes a large number of books by Jesuit writers with Franciscans close behind, and Benedictines, Carthusians and Carmelites well represented. As one would expect, apologetics written for the English situation, and drawn from the period of St John Fisher in the sixteenth century, Gother in the seventeenth, also figure largely. Among the many books of liturgical interest is the only known copy of the Norwich Missal from pre-Reformation times. The spiritual books include some very uncommon items on devotion to Our Lady, and on the Rosary.

Pullen refers to the Association of Staffordshire Clergy, the history of which 'may shed some light upon the way in which the Harvington Library grew to such a size'. The Association came into being about 1686 and one of its stated objectives was to 'have a public library or two in the county'. Every priest at his death was to leave part of his books to be placed in these libraries. However, it is to several Catholic families in the Midlands that one must also look as sources between 1619 and 1755. Lastly, of course, the arrival of Hugh Tootell (Charles Dodd), the priest historian, in Harvington in the early eighteenth century doubtless encouraged the accumulation of further volumes. Indicative of this is a massive dictionary in manuscript in two folio volumes, compiled by Dodd for the purposes of

*Spiritual Exercises* by Father Antonio de Molina, Carthusian monk of Miraflores, 1622. This work in Spanish bears the initials H. P. (Humphrey Pakington).

his *Church History*. This historical and critical work contains notices of the most eminent Catholics covering the period 1500–1688.

The removal of the library from Harvington can be traced to Bishop Milner who first wrote to the Harvington priest, John Corne, on 31 December 1806:[2]

> What is of greater importance is to get a list of the Books still remaining at Harvington, and belonging to the clergy, made out, and sent to me. In the mean time I hope you will keep them dusted and aired; and, those which were turned out into the passage, replaced in the Library.
>
> My intention is to come over as soon as I possibly can to see and examine them. I have reason to think many of them, though old, are of great value, having been collected by Mr Chs. Dodd ...

Milner was at Harvington for Confirmation towards the end of 1809 and in June of the following year took the opportunity of replying to John Corne's complaints about lack of sufficient income to mention the books again:

> I recollect desiring you to get the books belonging to the clergy of this District at Harvington put in order ... I have at the same time to inform you that Mr Potts [Thomas Potts (1754–1819) was President of old Oscott (i.e. present day Maryvale) Thomas Walsh (1776–1849) also on the staff of Oscott, was later Vicar Apostolic of the Midland District.] of his own accord and without any communication with me, applied some time ago to Sir John Throckmorton for his consent to remove the said Books from Harvington to Oscott, for his own use and that of the other Masters at the latter place, and that Sir John returned him for answer that he had no objection to the proposal. I, on my part, have said the same. Hence you may expect that Mr Walsh will, one of these days, send a cart over to Harvington to take away the said Books: but, in the mean time, Messrs Potts and Walsh beg you will take the first opportunity of sending them the catalogue of the Library, which they beg you will direct to the former to the care of <u>Mr Wilks Bookseller,</u> New Street, Birmingham. The said Genln. both desire their Compts. to you. I remain, Dr Sir, Your most faithfully humble Svt.
>
> J. Milner

Signatures of Elenor Brookesby and Mary Pakington in a spiritual treatise.
Elenor, a friend of the Jesuit Father Garnet, most probably took refuge at
Harvington after the Gunpowder Plot of 1605.

On 4 August 1810 Corne wrote at some length to the Oscott authorities:

> Memorandm. for the Gentn. at Oscott
> Much has been said about the Library books being sent off together
> with Mr Hartley's, at his death. I understand at the Hall, that Mr
> H's books were mostly new and well bound books, & they don't
> think that any Library books were intermixed. Old Miss Bagnall
> says, that when the Harvington stipend was lost in the French
> funds, Mr Vaughan the Pt. was greatly distressed, and leave was
> given him to make money of the Library books. Several of the
> Gentn as Sr. Walter Blount, Dr Blount, Mr Rayment, herself, &
> many took tickets at 5s. the Ticket.
> There were various description (sic) of books, English and French
> thus disposed of. It is in recollection, that many setts of Dr Dodd's
> Church History were thus disposed of, up & down the Kingdom
> about the time. But whether they came from the Harvington
> Library, the writer never enquired.

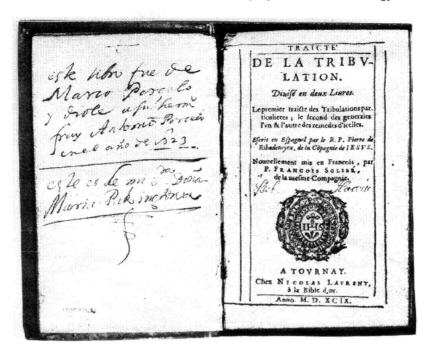

Mary Pakington was conversant with Spanish and French. This treatise on Tribulation is a French translation of the Jesuit, Ribadeneyra's work.

The writer, by order of Dr Milner, enquired at Gowers of Kidderminster, who understood many books belonging to Mr H had been sold there. He was shewn one Vol. of an elegant Quarto Breviary, for which sett 8gs. was asked. He saw 2 setts of lesser Breviaries; no price was affixed, nor would Mr Gower show the whole of the Lot he bought until the Inventory shd. be made out & he knew how to fix the prices by application to London for their value. When the writer called again Gower said, they were all sent off to London, as the best market. He supposed Dr Dodd's History, and the elegant Breviary would be bought for one of the Universities. When the writer replied to Dr Milner, he said as much of the above as he knew at the time of writing. The writer believes some articles were picked out by Mr Jas Parker of Stourport, and paid for to Mr Hartley's relations who were at Harvington at his Funeral, but not belonging to the Harv. Library. It is to be observed that Mr H probably succeeded to the Breviaries & books of his 2 uncles, who died not long before him in this District. The writer found no sett of Breviaries in the Library, only some odd, worn out, volumes. At the Bp's request to have the Library cleaned, he got Betty Long & her daughter to wipe every Book, & to dust the place, for which he paid 14.6d. He intended to have arranged them, but his eyes, & gouty habit did not permit. He found, however, after being 2 days in the Library, the greatest deficiencies of the Catalogue,[3] sent before the Books to Birm. according to Dr Milner's order. Till the writer came, it rained in upon the Books by places thro' the Roof, especially after snows, so that many Books stuck together. Many fragments of books were also in the Library half eaten away, & some also nearly ate by the rats and mice. The Tiles on the Roof were repaired, & the plaister replaced on the Library ceiling, & cats day and night kept in the house. So near the Water, it is very difficult to keep the water rats out. When Mr Cornthwaite came to this place, the Rats used to surround him while eating his Dinner: & thus before he came, the Books were destroyed wholesale. Mr Hartley had bad health, & nothing done in this time to clean the Library etc.

The writer laid a particular injunction on his Servants never to touch a Book, merely to sweep the Room. As far as lay in his power, the Books are as entire as he found them.

J. Corne

It is clear from this letter that the Library was situated on the upper floor where the chapels and the priests' rooms were also sited. In any case what is traditionally called Dr Dodd's Library could only have accommodated a fraction of the 1,729 books listed in the eighteenth-century Catalogue, and it is more likely that Dodd used the room as his study, keeping only the essential materials for his literary work there. Today the Harvington books now numbering about 1100 are well kept in the Recusant Library, and can be seen by students and researchers of this period.

---

[1]   G F Pullen, 'Recusant Books at St. Mary's, Oscott', Parts I & II (Oscott, 1964); see also 'The Harvington Library at Oscott,' *Worcester Recusant* 1, April 1963, pp. 18–20.

[2]   Correspondence originally in Oscott archives.

[3]   'An Index of all the books contained in the Library at Harvington belonging to the Secular Clergy. Begun Anno Domini May 10 1755.' Handwritten on paper and bound in vellum. BAA p168/5/1.

# 10

# THE SCHOOL

The story of education at Harvington begins with Arthur Vaughan, who came as chaplain to the Hall in 1752. Vaughan established a school for girls within the Hall itself and employed a teacher, Miss Ainsworth, to take charge. The school remained at Harvington until around 1778, when it moved to Oscott House, now known as Maryvale, and later closed.

The School, early 20th century.

When John Marsden took charge of the mission in 1816, he became dissatisfied with the situation whereby Catholic children attended the Protestant Charity Schools in Chaddesley Corbett and had to frequent the village church on certain occasions or be deprived of their education. He therefore approached Sir George Throckmorton, and with the help of Lady Throckmorton and others, set up a Catholic Free School in Harvington.

Exactly where the children were taught is not recorded – although it was most likely in the Hall. In any case the disastrous fire in 1823, which destroyed part of the Georgian Chapel, and the building of St Mary's Church soon afterwards, freed the Chapel, once it had been repaired, for its new use as a schoolroom. Under Sir Charles Throckmorton and Fr Brownlow the school began to thrive and was made available to the non-Catholic children of Harvington as well.

The list of communicants for 1822 mentions a John Howell, schoolmaster of Harvington. Gillow says that Howell later moved to Preston, Lancashire, and we know that the school's longest serving master, Joseph Ilsley, took up the post in 1827.[1] Ilsley came from a Midland Catholic family which was to provide Birmingham with its first archbishop, Edward Ilsley, who came to seek the peace and tranquility of Harvington's old Hall towards the end of his episcopacy. When Joseph Ilsley became schoolmaster he was merely twenty-one. Ten years later he married Isabella Hall and they lived in the rooms at the Hall. Joseph died aged sixty-nine in 1874, his wife having predeceased him by some years; they are buried side by side next to the path leading to the church door, Joseph's memorial recording his '43 years of faithful service' to the school.

Details for the earlier years of the school's existence are scarce, and even Brownlow merely alludes to the occasional celebratory tea parties, as for instance on 23 August 1860, he noted: 'having been 40 years a priest, I gave our schoolchildren, etc, a Tea-Drinking. "A very pleasant party" (£1.12.0).' There were probably a number of occasions when Brownlow turned to Ilsley for help, and when the priest became seriously ill in 1863 it was the schoolmaster who was despatched to bring the doctor.

By 1870 Fr Brownlow was complaining that a number of his younger people were moving to the towns, especially to Kidderminster and Wolverhampton, in search of employment. Ilsley's death about this time was another cause for concern about the future of the school. Miss Throckmorton came over from Coughton to discuss with the priest the possibility of employing a qualified teacher, but Brownlow rejected the idea as being too expensive. His retirement however enabled his successor, Fr Wilson, to give the school a new lease of life, and so the *Laity Directory* for Birmingham Diocese in 1885/6 records no less than forty-six scholars. Maria O'Sullivan was schoolmistress in the 1881 census.[2]

The last thirty years, 1885–1913, are the best documented, even though none of the log books, compulsory for State-inspected schools, has been found. The *Laity Directory* for Birmingham and Reports of the Diocesan School Inspector now provide evidence about teachers, number of children and grants received. There were two qualified teachers in the 1890s; Mary Kellard and Sarah Burke, and the number of children was generally around forty. These two teachers were followed by Mrs Castell and Mrs Harris. As the century drew to a close Catholic children became fewer, thirteen as compared with twenty to twenty-five non-Catholics, perhaps indicating a shift in the population of Harvington village from a Catholic majority to a non-Catholic one.

All non-Catholic pupils must have received a non-denominational religious education, whereas the Catholic children were additionally taught their faith to satisfy the School Board inspector and the Diocesan inspector. The Anglican *Catechism on Holy Scripture* by the Revd Edward James Phipps was in use at Harvington so as to comply with the General School Board regulation, 'that the Bible should be read and an explanation given therefrom in the principles of morality and religion as are suited to the capacity of children'. In addition, the Catholic children were examined by the Diocesan Inspector on prayers, catechism, doctrine and church history. Winifred Elwell taught the Catholics their religious knowledge.

In 1901 Catherine Burne appears as head teacher when the number of pupils attending was twenty-nine (only eight of them Catholics the previous year). Sir William Throckmorton wrote to Bishop Ilsley saying that he would only keep the school open for another year, the increased teachers' salaries and his declining interest in the Chaddesley properties which he was in the process of selling off being additional factors. Nevertheless, the school lingered on until midsummer 1913 when it closed 'for want of scholars', as Fr Roskell noted in his register. The schoolroom, where the teachers' rostrum had replaced the burnt altar and footpace of the one-time chapel, now became a lumber room until some seventy years later Archbishop Couve de Murville ordered its restoration as 'The Georgian Chapel'. Today it is in constant use for Mass by the parish and by various groups who come to the Hall for retreat days or sacramental preparations.

[1] J. Gillow, registers of Harvington CRS no. 17, 1915, p. 415.

[2] See Bauer, P., 'Roman Catholic Elementary Education in Victorian England' *Social History*, 1985.

# 11

# THE HARVINGTON PILGRIMAGE

The cultus of the English martyrs may be said to date from their own times. Relics of the martyrs were quickly secured (often at great danger) by devout Catholics and treasured throughout Penal Days; representations of their barbaric executions were also painted for the Venerable English College in Rome from which many of the 'seminary priests' came. Yet liturgical recognition could not be given until beatification and canonization – a stage only reached towards the close of the nineteenth century and in many cases not until our own day.

It has been noted with surprise that Charles Dodd, Harvington's priest and notable church historian, made only a modest reference to the mission's own martyr, John Wall; also, that in his many surviving sermons Dodd makes no allusion to martyrdom.[1] Perhaps this reticence can be partly explained by the fact that Dodd was writing in the early years of the eighteenth century. Certainly, in the following century John Brownlow was fully aware of his parish's honour in being associated with the labours and heroic death of his seventeenth-century predecessor. It was William Wilson, who succeeded Brownlow, who decided to mark the two hundredth anniversary of Wall's martyrdom by erecting a large stone cross suitably inscribed in the centre of St Mary's churchyard. Again some years later Fr Roskell speaks with pride in one of his sermons on Harvington's long Catholic history and its martyr, but we have to wait for the restoration of the Hall to begin, with the beatification of John Wall in 1929, before the idea of a diocesan pilgrimage was mooted.

In the *Diocesan Year Book* for 1931 Fr Alfred Whittington, Roskell's successor, wrote that

> our chief interest at Harvington is not the mere preservation of the fabric of the old mansion, rather it is its connection with the stren-

The Harvington Pilgrimage, *c.*1949.

uous times of persecution through which this country passed from 1532 to 1680, and the fact that one of its priests, Father John Wall, O.S.F., was hung, drawn and quartered at Worcester for the faith on August 22, 1679 ... Our intention is not to be content with chance visitors and sightseers, however. We want something very much better than that. We want pilgrimages, in the truest sense of the word, both diocesan and parochial, throughout the year to honour our Midland Martyrs. For Harvington is the shrine not only of Blessed John Wall, but of all the Blessed Martyrs who gave their lives for the faith that we in this twentieth century might have the consolations of our holy religion.

Fr Whittington then went on to inform his readers that Harvington was being made into the shrine of all the martyrs where Mass could be offered on all their feasts with special ceremony, their cult revived and spread throughout the diocese.

The pilgrimages, he announced, had already begun, and on 22 August 1930 the archbishop led the first annual diocesan pilgrimage. It was a success, though hampered by the ruinous state of the Hall. The following year the pilgrimage was repeated:

> ... beginning with Mass for the first time in the restored secret chapel. Although the little church was comfortably full at the principal and Solemn High Mass, it cannot be said with truth that the assembly anything like represented the gathering of the faithful which ought to have been there. Certainly there were excuses: the weather, the holiday season, the day itself – a Saturday – must have kept many people away. But the fact remains that if one town, Stourbridge, had not figured largely in the proceedings, the gathering to honour the Martyrs and receive our Archbishop would have been a small one indeed.

More encouraging were the parochial pilgrimages to Harvington throughout the year. These were no mere sightseeing outings but real acts of devotion in which prayers were recited, an address on the martyrs given, the relic of St John Wall venerated and the whole concluded with Benediction.

On the eve of the war in 1939 the pilgrimage was still linked with the feast of St John Wall. There was Mass at 8.00 a.m. in the Hall chapel with Solemn High Mass at 11.30 a.m. in the Great Chamber. Benediction at 2.30 p.m. in church and veneration of the relics. By

1941 this had been reduced to an 8.30 a.m. Mass at the Hall and evening Benediction in the church.

When Fr Crichton came, the celebration in honour of the martyr was observed by a rally on the nearest Sunday and an address by the auxiliary, Bishop Humphrey Bright, at 4.00 p.m. A procession and Benediction closed the evening. At the 1952 Sunday pilgrimage the Bishop of Plymouth, Mgr Grimshaw, soon to be translated to Birmingham, gave the address with the procession and Benediction following at 6.30 p.m. This remained the pattern for many years, until in fact it became possible to have Mass at a time other than the morning.

In more recent years the Pilgrimage Mass has taken place at 3.00 p.m. with the archbishop or assistant bishop usually acting as principal celebrant together with some twenty-five concelebrants and several deacons from nearby parishes. Numbers attending the Pilgrimages have increased over the years and are between six and eight hundred. The Mass takes place on a raised and canopied scaffold in the grounds of the Hall and the house is open for pilgrims afterwards, without charge, in recognition of the diocese's continuing financial support.

[1] Dodd however records the deaths of the martyrs, including that of Francis Johnston (John Wall) *Church History* vol. 3, p. 311.

# 12

# THE HARVINGTON FESTIVAL

The Harvington Festival, now a firmly established event, was the brainchild of Janet Arbuthnott, of Winterfold School, and Fr Geoffrey Tucker. Mrs Arbuthnott, wife of Winterfold's headmaster and parish organist for some years, conceived the idea of promoting cultural activities in relation to Harvington Hall. The Hall's Elizabethan setting naturally suggested early music and drama, and this characterised the festival during its first years. The first festival took place in 1983 and was limited to two days, 9 and 10 July, later extended to cover two weekends. On the Saturday evening 'St Mary's Ecumenical Choir' (presumably the parish choir was augmented by Anglicans and others) sang sixteenth- and seventeenth-century motets. A talk, 'Harvington Hall through the ages', was given by Michael Hodgetts, and the Orlando Consort played music for flutes, virginals and lutes. A running buffet and wine bar was open from 6.00 p.m. On the next day the organist of St Chad's Cathedral, David Saint, gave a recital in the village church which was followed by High Mass celebrated by the Archbishop of Birmingham, Maurice Couve de Murville, with music sung by the cathedral choir. In the Hall gardens the boys of Winterfold gave a performance of *A Man for all Seasons*. Evensong in St Mary's and seventeenth-century dancing and madrigals followed, to be brought to an end by the customary buffet and wine bar.

By 1986 the festival had acquired two musical patrons, Emma Kirkby and Anthony Rooley, proudly announced as 'leading exponents of early Music'; West Midlands Arts were also giving their support. Compared with the first festival, that of 1986 was more ambitious, exhaustive and probably exhausting. The Choir of Magdalene College, Oxford, sang in St Cassian's, Chaddesley, at 3.00 p.m. to be followed by Vespers. 'Music from the Towers', an annual brass band event in the grounds of James Arbuthnott's Stone Cottage, could then be heard at 6.30 p.m. or if preferred, one could then go on at 7.00 p.m. to hear more Early Music sung by the New London Consort in St Mary's Church. A no-doubt much appreciated buffet supper and reception at 9.00 p.m. brought the day to a close. On Sunday an organ recital preceded the 12 noon 'High Mass' at which the visiting choir performed polyphony and chant, and the sermon was given by a special preacher, on this occasion Mgr J. D. Crichton, Harvington's former parish priest and notable liturgist, returned to speak. In the afternoon actors from the Crescent Theatre, Birmingham, performed extracts from Shakespeare, together with songs and dancing in the garden of the Hall. At 5.30 p.m. an Anglican Evensong was sung in St Mary's by St Chad's singers, the precentor of Worcester Cathedral leading, and the Bishop of Dudley preaching. Light refreshments and wine were available at 7.00 p.m. followed by the York Waits and the Gobbi Players. Again a buffet supper and reception ended the long day. Early Music, it has to be said, appeals to a limited audience and while local music critics extolled the festival as a cultural gem it could also be said, as in 1987, 'the programme on the whole was still hard listening'. Despite widespread publicity and big names like Emma Kirkby and Ian Partridge, the concerts never made any profit, nor did they attract parishioners.

The standard was extremely high, the refreshments truly delicious – the menu for 18 July 1992 tempted the palate with such items as 'Honey glazed ham with apricots and caraway, brichettes of chicken marinated in green spices, home smoked salmon on rye bread', all calculated to draw a somewhat highbrow clientèle.

As it will have been noted, venues other than the Hall were found to be necessary; St Mary's Church had the advantage of providing more seating than the Hall, although church benches are notoriously uncomfortable for any length of time, and those in St Mary's were laboriously replaced for the concert with chairs. Winterfold School Hall was also used for a few years and provided a more appropriate setting in 1993 for 'Hot Stuff', a traditional Jazz Band, an innovation in startling contrast to 'Courtly Musick' in the Hall's Great Chamber.

The Festival's founders have passed away but its committee composed of members of the parish continues to provide cultural uplift every July which is no longer confined to early music.

# 13

# THE ALMSHOUSES AND APPRENTICESHIPS

As Lady of the Manor throughout the last half of the seventeenth century, Dame Mary Yate was concerned with the common good of her dependents and their families. This took the very practical form of the establishment in 1674 of almshouses in Harvington for three poor widows and the provision of grants for training apprentices from among the poor children of the village. Various properties and pieces of land in the locality and even further afield in such places as Droitwich, Salwarpe, Madresfield and Great Malvern were acquired and rented out to ensure the perpetuity of these charities.[1]

The Almshouses before the rebuilding.

In the 1830s the almshouse properties consisted of nineteen acres in Harvington itself with each of the poor widows receiving a pension of £9 per annum. The almshouses were kept in repair out of the funds and the accounts were duly submitted to the then lord of the manor and audited by him; the trustees were usually local landowners, friends, and the vicar of St Cassians's.

At the same period the property for supporting the apprentices consisted of twenty acres of land in Harvington and Cakebole and enclosed in five or six fields, together with a small cottage. The closes were occupied by tenants. Five houses and other properties in Droitwich and Salwarpe were still bringing in further rents at this date.

Around 1858 Sir Robert Throckmorton erected a fourth almshouse and embellished each dwelling with the family coat of arms carved in stone. By the early twentieth century the inhabitants were receiving pensions of £4 10s a quarter with a little extra for coal, but the old buildings on the corner of Morton Road were by this time deemed beyond improvement. To support the application for their demolition it was pointed out that they had no separate WC accommodation but only insanitary pail closets; no proper drainage system, no scullery or adequate cooking arrangements, uneven tiled floors and inadequate lighting. The replacement almshouses of 1962, standing further back from the lane, are perhaps less interesting but undoubtedly more comfortable for the widows, who now mostly come from beyond the parish boundaries of Chaddesley Corbett. In 1924 the charity was still offering 'help with the local children's education and secondary schools, assisting boys and girls in their emigration expenses, making grants to Chaddesley Nursing Fund and in increasing annuities to Almshouse widows', but seemingly the last grant was made in 1931.

[1] HPA

# 14

# BADGE COURT, PURSHALL HALL, HARBOROUGH HALL AND WARESLEY HOUSE

## BADGE COURT

The Harvington mission was of considerable importance in the seventeenth and eighteenth centuries, but it was one of a number of such Mass centres in this particularly Catholic corner of Worcestershire. While Harvington was probably served by the secular clergy for most of its early and certainly its later history, the Franciscans and Jesuits were active elsewhere. Thus Grafton Manor (the home of the Shrewsbury Talbots) and the neighbouring houses of Badge Court and Purshall Hall were Jesuit strongholds, as indeed was Worcester itself.[1]

Badge Court near Elmbridge was a Talbot property, coming into the Wintour family towards the end of the sixteenth century along with Huddington. It was here that Helen, daughter of Robert Wintour of Huddington and one of the Gunpowder Plot conspirators, lived. Helen's mother was Gertrude, daughter of Sir John Talbot of Grafton, near Bromsgrove.

Her father, Robert, was executed in 1606, but Helen lived on at Badge Court for many years, spending many of her leisure hours embroidering exquisite vestments to be used in her chapel above the stairs. Some of her work can still be seen today in the museum at Stonyhurst.

After Helen's death the Talbots farmed the property out to tenants until it was eventually sold in 1925. In the course of time the timber-framed manor house underwent many alterations and with the sale sadly lost its most beautiful features – its panelling, carvings and splendid heraldic glass, all of which is now in Cumberland Lodge in Windsor Great Park. The spacious chapel (now a bedroom) has an aumbry next to the fireplace and what may have been a secret hiding-place. In front of the house is a large pond, the remains of a moat which was largely filled in many years ago. In 1734 Grafton and Badge Court were served by Fr Charles Piercy. Afterwards Badge Court came under the care of Fr Thomas Weldon, while Grafton was given to his brother, Fr James Weldon. When James left Grafton both missions were served by Thomas, until once more united under Fr John Baynham. In 1742 Baynham transferred the Mass centre to Purshall Hall, a neighbouring farm of which his sister was a tenant and where he continued to live until his death.

## PURSHALL HALL

Purshall Hall can be seen across the fields from Badge Court and is a large timber-framed building faced with brick. It mostly dates from the Jacobean period. The Hall was owned by the Purshall family from the thirteenth to the eighteenth centuries, but apart from Magdalen, wife of James Purshall, who appears in the Churchwardens' Presentments of the Elmbridge parish (1671–1684), the family does not seem to have been Catholic, unless there were later converts. In the attic was a chapel which Fr Baynham used when he first moved in; this was furnished with a wooden altar and altar rails the origins of which are disputed. What is certain is that the priest celebrated Mass at this altar for many years, and that in the 1940s H. R. Hodgkinson attempted to have it transferred to Harvington but was prevented by the Rev W. Sterry-Cooper, vicar of Elmbridge, who persuaded the owner to let him place the furniture in his own church where – much restored – it can still be seen.

In 1795 Fr Baynham upset Lord Shrewsbury by some remark about the monks of La Trappe whom he, at Shrewsbury's request, was temporarily accommodating in Purshall Hall. Like a number of refugees from the Revolution, the French clergy and religious were dependent on the charity of their English co-religionists for shelter and some measure of support. The outcome of Baynham's quarrel is not known, and the Jesuit died soon after. The Hall was then purchased by the Wakemans of Little Malvern Court, an old Catholic family, so that the chapel may have continued in use into the early 1800s.[2]

## HARBOROUGH HALL

Yet another house in the present parish of Harvington is Harborough Hall, Blakedown. This is a timber-framed building dating from the late sixteenth century, whose occupant, Roger Pen, married Margaret Pakington at Chaddesley Corbett in 1590. She was convicted of recusancy shortly afterwards as one of 'the gentlewomen that refuse the church though their husbands do not.'

Two hiding places for priests were said to have existed here, although one of them seems to have been simply for books.[3]

[1] Camm, *Forgotten Shrines*, pp. 269–75; Aileen Hodgeson, 'The Chapel and Mission of Grafton Manor 1218–1874', *Worcestershire Recusant* 9, Dec. 1966.

[2] T G Holt, SJ, 'Purshall Hall and Fr John Baynham', *Worcestershire Recusant*, 15, June 1970.

[3] Lionel and Veronica Webster, 'The Pakingtons of Harvington', Recusant History, 12, no. 5, April 1974, p. 206.

Alan Fea, *Secret Chambers and Hiding Places*, Bouspel, 1904; Michael Hodgetts, *Secret Hiding Places*, Oscott series 3, 1989.

## WARESLEY HOUSE

Standing in what remains of a park in Hartlebury, and now cheek-by-jowl with a modern housing estate, is a large old house which was for a number of years used as an Approved School for boys. The house was built by John Baker in the late eighteenth century and had a varied history. In the mid-nineteenth century it was let to John Peel, Dean of Worcester (1845–1874), brother of Robert Peel, the prime minister. In 1920 the house was purchased by Captain Allan Dyson Perrins, whose wife was a notable hostess. The family continued to live there until the end of the Second World War when the property was taken by the De La Salle Brothers, a teaching order, who moved their school from Brandon in Suffolk. St Gilbert's, as it was known, had its own chapel and chaplain and was not under the care of Harvington parish.[1]

Brother Augustine, the headmaster, encouraged the boys to participate in village events: in 1952 a new village hall was built by volunteers to celebrate the accession of Queen Elizabeth II and the boys helped particularly with the digging out of the foundations. With the expansion of Hartlebury after the war many new Catholic families came to live in the village. Ronald Fry, a Harvington parishioner and chairman of governors of St Gilbert's, then suggested that Fr McGovern, the chaplain, should make the chapel available on Sundays for those people who had no means of transport for getting to Harvington or Kidderminster. This arrangement continued until the school closed in the 1970s, when, as with the majority of such institutions run by religious, their numbers were decimated by the 'wind of change' that swept through communities in the wake of the Second Vatican Council.

[1] R. O. Walker, *Hartlebury, A Record of a Parish*, pp. 61–3.

# APPENDIX I[1]
# MEMORIAL INSCRIPTIONS IN
# ST MARY'S CHURCHYARD

Names given in alphabetical order. Letters and numbers refer to rows.

E6      **Hugh Forbes Arbuthnott** of Winterfold House 1906–1982
        Laus Deo
        **Janet Elizabeth Arbuthnott** 1915–1990 Organist of this
        parish 1949–1989

St Mary's churchyard.

*Organ*   To the memory of Janet Arbuthnott organist at this church for nearly 40 years until 1990
Make a joyful noise unto the Lord.

B5      **Randle Bagnall** died May 31<sup>st</sup> 1842 aged 76 years
B6      **Martha Bagnall** his wife died March 24<sup>th</sup> 1838 RIP

12      **Father Thomas Vincent Bagnall** 1898–1973 Parish Priest of St Mary's, Harvington 1955–1968 May he rest in peace and **Helen Marie Bagnall** his sister 1896–1983 May she rest in peace.

E5      In loving memory of a devoted husband **Joseph Anthony Bashford (Tony)**
28 8 1920–23 12 1983 RIP and ever loving wife **Elizabeth May Bashford** 4.5.1921–30.1.2005 RIP

D2b    Of your charity pray for the soul of **Helen Bayley** who died Jan 8 1931 aged 67 ever faithful. Also of her sister **Elizabeth Bayley** died March 1933 aged 77 RIP

*East Wall*
      **Sophie Beard** 17.8.1976–24.11.1976 RIP

C8      **? Charles Broad ?** 1838
*(There is a headstone, but surface completely flaked off so illegible)*

B13     Oct 27<sup>th</sup> aged 74 years 1852 **Martha Gibs** *(broken, 2 pieces)*

B14     IHS of your charity pray for the repose of the soul of the **Revd John Brownlow** priest of this mission 51 years who departed this life March 14 1888 aged 93 years on whose soul sweet Jesus have mercy RIP

D21     Of your charity pray for the soul of **Elizabeth Buckley** who departed this life April 21<sup>st</sup> 1863 aged 75 years.
*East Wall*
      Treasured memories of **Bob Bullock** born 13.10.1925 – died 12.7.1996
      **Faye Bullock** born 3.8.1922 – died 12.4.1999

*East Wall*

In loving memory of **Bernard Campbell** died 26th Oct 2001 aged 82 years

|17      Of your charity pray for the soul of **Elizabeth Chare** who died Jan 24 1906 aged 81 years. On whose soul sweet Jesus have mercy Also of **Agnes Christina Chare** who died March 30 1912 in her 85$^{th}$ year RIP

|18      Of your charity pray for the soul of **Joseph Chare** who died at Chaddesley Corbett 16 March 1865 aged 80 years. On whose soul sweet Jesus have mercy. Amen.
Also of **Helen Chare** daughter of Robert and Elizabeth Chare who died July 28 1899 aged 88 years RIP

B16     IHS Of your charity of your mercy pray for the repose of the soul of **Maria Lucy Chare** who died April 20$^{th}$ 1898 aged 75 years RIP

|15      Pray for the repose of the soul of **Robert Chare** who died 12 May 1859 aged 72 years.

|16      Also of **Elizabeth** wife of the above who died September 4$^{th}$ 1883 aged 80 (86)? years.

|5       In loving memory of **Mary Monica Connelly** Born Sep 7$^{th}$ 1885 died Feb 3$^{rd}$ 1975

C9      Of your charity pray *(for the soul of)* **Joseph Thomas Corbett** w . . . . . . . . . 1927 aged 79
. . . . . . . . . . . . . . . **Harriet** beloved wife of the above died July 25$^{th}$ 1952 aged 89 years RIP

A3      In loving memory of **Isabel Helen Cox** died May 29$^{th}$ 1939 aged 78 years.

F1      In loving memory of a dear husband and father, **George David Darby** died May 24$^{th}$ 1967 aged 80 years, also of his dear wife **Agnes Mary**, died August 15$^{th}$ 1972 aged 89 years.

A18    To the dear memory of **John**, second son of Richard and Etheldreda **Davenhill**, born Jan 4 1935, died Nov 24 1935 RIP

In loving memory of **Richard Eric (Peter) Davenhill** of Pedmore Worcs Jan 21<sup>st</sup> 1898–Feb 8<sup>th</sup> 1961, beloved husband of Reda dear father of Tony, John & Richard. Also his devoted wife **Reda** Jan 8<sup>th</sup> 1905–April 23 1998 On whose souls sweet Jesus have mercy.

J1    Pray for the soul of **R E M Davidson** born 4<sup>th</sup> February 1893, died August 1933.
Eternal rest give unto them O Lord

J9    Pray for the repose of the soul of **Agnes Mary Drinkwater** of Beausale who died February 24<sup>th</sup> 1939 aged 83 years, also of her sister **Katherine Mary Drinkwater** who died July 4<sup>th</sup> 1939 aged 83 years RIP

|24    Laus Deo – Baby **Joseph** son of Henry & Gladys **Drinkwater** Born & died July 16 1916

|23    Of your charity pray for the soul of **Katharine Winifrede** daughter of TG & A **Drinkwater** (The Mearse) who died Aug 24 1900 aged 16

|22    RIP Of your charity pray for the soul of **Thomas George Drinkwater** (of The Mearse) who died November 18, 1916 aged 68 years, also of **Alice** his wife who died January 25 1936 aged 80 years.

|21    Of your charity pray for the soul of **Julian Aloysius Drinkwater** died October 4<sup>th</sup> 1948 aged 89 years.
Fortified with the rites of Holy Church RIP

E1    Pray for the soul of **Charles Edward Eagle** DD for 12 years parish priest of Harvington who died Nov 26<sup>th</sup> 1947 aged 66 years fortified with Holy Rites of Holy Church.

D14    IHS **Joseph Elwell** of Blakedown who died March 11<sup>th</sup> 1909 aged 61 years may he rest in peace.

J20    Of your charity pray for the soul of **Joseph Elwell** who died December 8<sup>th</sup> 1933 in his 60<sup>th</sup> year. On whose soul Sweet Jesus have mercy.

D2      RIP In loving memory of our dear mother **Mary Elizabeth Elwell** died Nov 23$^{rd}$ 1918 aged 75 years.

D22      Of your charity pray for the soul of **Samuel John Elwell** who died April 23$^{rd}$ 1920 aged 67 years also of **Lucy** his wife who died Feb 27$^{th}$ 1925 aged 74 years RIP

         **Emery** see Whitehouse Ann

A7/11      In loving memory of **Patrick Joseph Farrell** died 11$^{th}$ March 1951 aged 55
Also in memory of the late **Agnes Matilda Farrell** born April 1901 and died 11$^{th}$ June 1982

J4/5      Remember **Ellen Ferris** who gave Harvington Hall to Holy Church died 5$^{th}$ September 1955 aged 85 & her only son **Sir Robert Grant Grant-Ferris**, Baron Harvington AEPC of Nantwich, Cheshire, Knight of Malta, Deputy Speaker House of Commons 1970–1974. Died New Year's Day 1997 aged 89
May they rest in peace waiting for the day of resurrection.

J2      I am the Immaculate Conception
Of your charity pray for the repose of the soul of **William Foster Fletcher** who died Jan 11$^{th}$ 1946 aged 80 years. Also his wife **Mary Winifrede** who died Dec 16$^{th}$ 1956 aged 88 years. Eternal rest grant unto them O Lord, and let perpetual light shine upon them. (Also buried here are the ashes of **Elizabeth Eardley** who died 15$^{th}$ April 2002 aged 83)

E3      In memory of **John L. Ford** died 25 Nov 1953 aged 57
Also of his wife **Ethel Evelyn** died 31 Oct 1981 aged 79

F14      Pray for **Margaret Fryer** Born 25 August 1921 Died 14$^{th}$ May 1977

*Wall*      In everlasting memory of a cherished husband and father **Kevin James Gallagher**
02 09 56 – 27 11 02 aged 46 RIP

C6      In memory of **Anthony Thomas Goodyear** Our beloved

Tony 4/2/1934 28/2/1988
From good men goodness may be learnt.

H1      RIP **Elizabeth Mary Grant** 1906–1970 – **Clive Gilbert Grant** 1941–1980
        **Francis Denis Grant** 1903–1990

*Wall*    **Lilian Elizabeth Grant** died 28th August 1987 aged 71 years. Rest in Peace

H17     267040 Private G **Griffin** Royal Warwickshire Regiment 5th May 1919 aged 22
        Rest in Peace

J16/17  In loving memory of **George Griffin** who entered into rest March 20th 1896 aged 59 years On whose soul sweet Jesus have mercy RIP Also of **Sarah Griffin** wife of the above who entered into rest Oct . . . . . . . . . . . . . . *(stone flaking)*

C13     Of your charity pray for the soul of **Maria Griffin** who departed this life August 26 1878 aged 86 RIP. May she rest in peace.

F13     Pray for the repose of the souls of **Barbara Winifred** and **Agnes Hailes** died 1881 RIP
        *(Log-like cross and wreath on rocky outcrop, scroll on stones with lilies)*

|14     RIP Of your charity pray for the soul of **Edward M Hailes** who died Dec 11 1912 aged 55 years also of **Anne Mary** his wife who died 13 May 1924

E10     Of your charity pray for the repose of the soul of **Edward Hailes** who died December 1896 aged 83 also of **Edward Thomas Hailes** of Harvington born November 6th 1889, died April 1955. Grandson of Edward Hailes.

E11     Of your charity pray for the repose of the soul of **Elizabeth Hailes** of Harvington who departed this life October 16th 1881 aged 65. On whose soul Sweet Jesus have mercy RIP Also of **Joseph Hailes** who died September 27th 1894 aged 21 RIP

H8   Sacred to the memory of **James Hanbury** a native of Tallow – County of Waterford, Ireland who died in Kidderminster Oct 10th 1831 aged 19 years. Also of **Michael Hanbury** brother of the above who died March 1838 aged ...... years RIP

**Harper** see Moore

|10   Pray for the soul of The **Rev C I Harris** (17 years Priest of Harvington) who died at Kidderminster April 10, 1905.

B2/3   Pray for the repose of the soul of **Maria Harris** late of Hartlebury who died at Harvington Hall Oct 30th 1913 aged 88 years. Also for **William Arthur** second son of the above who died May 1st 1901 aged 45 RIP

B15   Jesus mercy, Mary help. In memoriam **Philip Alfred Haskew** died March 1st 1897 aged 69 years RIP Also of **Mary Ann Haskew** wife of the above who died March 24th 1904 *(2 pieces)*

*Wall*   **Joseph Haydon** 1922–27th September 2000
**Grace Haydon** 1924–2004 Goodnight God Bless RIP

F8   In loving memory of a devoted couple **Joy Hayes** died 5 June 1996 aged 79 also **Peter (Louis) Hayes** died 23 November 1996 aged 65 Requiescat in Pace

C12   Pray for the soul of **John Hayward** who died July 25th 1907 aged 77 years also of **Jane** his wife who died April 4th 1926 aged 90 years fortified by the rites of Holy Church

D6b   Please pray for the soul of **Henry Hayward** born 27th Dec 1868 died 27th April 1949 Requiescat in Pace

*The Hall*
This avenue of yew trees was planted in 2003 with the support of the 'Friendship Group' in memory of their dear friend **Robert Hildebrandt**

B8/9   ................. of your ........... pray ...........

.... of ........ John H ...... n ........ who departed
this life at Harvi*(ngton?)* ........ aged ........ also of ...
.... wife ..... wife ...... Jesus, Mercy, Mary ..... on
her ......?. **John Hodgson** 6 March 1852 aged 66, **Elizabeth Hodgson** 1878 aged 86 *(stone badly damaged)*

J11   IHS Of your charity pray for the soul of **Isabella Ilsley** deceased November 28th 1860 aged 66 years. May she rest in peace.

J10   Of your charity pray for the soul of **Joseph Ilsley** for 43 years the faithful and respected Schoolmaster of Harvington he departed this life 20th July 1874 aged 69 years. On whose soul Sweet Jesus have mercy RIP

*Wall*   In loving memory of **Fr L W Jones** DD PhD BSc (Wallace) Priest of this parish 1969–1975 who died June 18th 1993 aged 88 and whose ashes are buried beneath this stone. May he rest in peace.

D4   **Maureen Kathleen Joseph** 24 11 86, **Henry Barnet Joseph** KSG 16 8 97

*or*
E

J6   In loving memory of a dear husband and father **Charles Keefe** died 18th January 1977 aged 66 years, Peace, perfect peace. And his beloved wife **Alice Patricia Keefe** 1908–1998 RIP

*Wall*   In loving memory of **Eileen (Bunny) Keenan** 25.8.1910–31.8.1995

|1   **Father Joseph Lacy** (Drumlish, Ireland) Parish Priest St. Mary's Harvington 1975–1978, born 21.10.1925, died 30.5.1978

F9a   Pray for the soul of **Ann Lewis** died Nov 25th 1842 aged 69 years RIP **William Lewis** died July 17th 1873 aged 73. Pray for the repose of the soul of **Mary** wife of William **Lewis** died Sept 6th 1887 aged 60 years.

A1       To the memory of **Mary Loftus** who died August 24<sup>th</sup> 1944 aged 24 years. Pray for the repose of her soul.

|3       Pray for the soul of **Philip Nicholas Lynch** Born 23 July 1907 Died 23 October 1973 and his wife **Rose Mary** Born 8 February 1913 died 23 April 1976

H7       In loving memory of **Pietro** beloved son of Rocco & Maria **Macchia** who died Sep 19, 1951 aged 17 years. May he rest in peace.

B12      **James Mackrell** died 27 October 1848 *(stone badly damaged and almost illegible)*

G1       Of your charity pray for the repose of the soul of **Angus Denys Maguire** who died Sep 9<sup>th</sup> 1962 aged 54 years Requiescat in Pace also in loving memory of **Joyce Kathleen Maguire** who joined her husband in Heaven on Sep 29<sup>th</sup> 1988 may they both rest in peace.

*Wall*    **Pauline Mary Mahon** born 22<sup>nd</sup> ....... 1926 died 11<sup>th</sup> Oct 1995

E9       Sacred memory of **Bernard Manning** who departed this life December 1835 in the 20<sup>th</sup> year of his life RIP

B9       In loving memory of **Bernard McKay** of Fir Tree Farm. A much loved husband and dear Daddy. Tragically killed Sept 20<sup>th</sup> 1985 aged 40 Love one another as I have loved you.

F4       **Siobhan McMahon** 1968–1969 For death is but an horizon and an horizon is nothing save the limit of our sight *(Headstone has an angel)*

A17      Of your charity, pray for the soul of **Agnes Mary** widow of **Robert Matthews** who died June 4<sup>th</sup> 1938 aged 62 years. On whose soul Sweet Jesus have mercy.

|8       Of your charity pray for the soul of **Maria Meek** who died March 28<sup>th</sup> 1888 aged 62 years. On whose soul Sweet Jesus have mercy.

H9      This stone was erected to the memory of **Mary Ann Molloy** who departed this life June 18 *(4?)* 5 aged 13 years and ? months

B1      IHS Of your charity pray for the repose of the soul of **Mary Helen** beloved wife of Felix James **Moore** of Wolverhampton. Who departed this life Nov 9. May she rest in peace.

*Wall*    In loving memory of **Mary Elizabeth Mullard** 15.1.1998 Quis Separabit

C7      Of your charity pray for the repose of the souls of **Mary Mulloy** died 1 Oct 1956 aged 88. On whose souls sweet Jesus have mercy *(on kerb stone?)*

*Organ*    Restored June 1925 in memoriam **Laurence Ruck & John Munster** killed in the Great War RIP

*Wall*    In memory of **Mary Murray** 30.11.1938–23.04.2003. Loving wife and mother.

*Wall*    Loving memories of **Anna Mary Newton** A wonderful mother and best friend Always in our thoughts. 19.8.1936–11.3.1992

D13     In memory of **Catherine** wife of **Thomas Nicholls** of Harvington who departed this life on 11th march in the year of our Lord 1839 And of the above named **Thomas Nicholls** who died Dec 30th 1856 aged ?

|19     Of your charity pray for the soul of **William Benedict Oakley** who departed this life March 1st 1908 aged 30 years. Sweet Heart of Mary be his salvation.

*Wall*    In loving memory of **Gerard A. O'Keeffe** died 21 2 03 aged 78 years RIP

       **Packwood** see Richards

C14?    of your charity pray for the soul of **George Parker**? late of Worcestershire aged 49, 1880? RIP

C2    Erected by her husband and children in affectionate remembrance of **Ann Parkes** late of Harvington Worcestershire who departed this life March 3<sup>rd</sup> 1863 aged 63 years.

C3    In charity pray for the soul of **Thomas Parkes** of Harvington who died August 25, 1872 aged 79 years. My soul hath relied on his word, my soul hath hoped on the Lord ... Psalm CXXIX My Jesus mercy RIP

C1?    *name unreadable, only* aged 41 *can be read, but grave stone has a cross and anchor* **Thomas Parkes**?

|3    Pray for the repose of the soul of **Brig-General Stanhope Humphrey Pedley** CBOL, Late Royal West Kent Regiment who died 17<sup>th</sup> February 1938, also of his wife **Mary Leonie** who died 23 October 1957 RIP

C4    In loving memory **Alice Mary Petre** died Dec 3<sup>rd</sup> 1921 RIP *(kerb only)*

E7    **Cyril William Joseph Radcliffe** Knight of Malta 1902–1981
**Joan Radcliffe** 1902–1983 beloved husband and wife.

E5    **James Reddan** Limerick 1833 *(stone by wall)*

*Wall*    Loving memories of **Mary Richards** nee Packwood 1912–2003 wife of **Stan** and Mary's twin sister **Josie** 1912–2004 RIP

*Wall*    Treasured memories of **Maureen Riley** died Oct 3<sup>rd</sup> 2003 aged 61 RIP

*Wall*    **Rochford** 1899 SW **(Sammy)** 1978, 1904 MT **(Molly)** 1990 RIP

B7    Treasured memories of **Chrissie Rose** 14–11–1918–12–11 –1991 Always in our thoughts. Also her beloved husband **Ralph** 27-8-1917 – 11-1-1997

F2    Pray for the soul of **Rev Philip George Roskell** parish

priest of Harvington 1900 –1930 Died Nov 25 1930 aged
71. Dulcis Anima Requiescat in Pace *'In loving memory'*

**Saunders** see Mulloy

*Wall*      **Eve Mary Smith** 1912–2001 RIP

|12      Of your charity pray for the repose of the soul of **Charles
Spink** of Harvington who died on Christmas Eeve 1885
aged 69 years. On whose soul Sweet Jesus have mercy RIP
. . . . . . the repose of the soul . . . . . . **Anne** wife of **Charles
Spink** who died October 1894? aged 64? . . . . . . . . RIP

*In church*

HSE **Gulielmus Ioannis F Trafford** qui diutino morbo
fortiter tolerato decessit XII Kal Septemb a MDCCCXXIX
quum uixisset annos XLVII Maria Trafford heres usufruc-
tuaria marito amantissimo concordissimo cum lacrimis oh
utinam quos mors disiunxit dura perenni in caelis iterum
foedere iungat amor RIP

*In church*

Pray for the repose of the soul of **William de Trafford** of
Pleremore, Worcestershire who died July 2nd 1901 aged 77
years RIP

E3a      **Philip Thomas Thatcher** born 28th January 1968 dies 11th
October 1968 Suffer little children to come unto me.

*Bench*      As you sit and rest a while remember me and all your loved
ones – dedicated to the memory of **Jenny Thompson** – with
fondest love from the Flower Ladies of St Mary's Harvington.

*East Wall*

***Father Geoffrey Robert Tucker*** 10 April 1919–21 June
1999
Beloved Parish Priest St Mary's Harvington 1978–1999 He
left this world a happier place.

*Churchyard Cross*
E8      **Fr John Wall** OSF in religion. Father Joachim of St Anne
who obeying God, rather than man for 12 years ministering

the sacraments to the faithful in this and other parts of Worcestershire in danger of death. He was born in 1620, ordained priest in 1645, professed OSF January 1652, was taken at Rushock Court December 1678 and put to death for the faith at Worcester on the Octave of the Assumption 1679. Beatified by Pope Pius XI December 15 1929. Canonised by Pope Paul VI 1970. This monument was restored to celebrate the Beatification of the 85 English Martyrs by Pope John Paul II November 22 1987.

*Wall*          **Vivienne Wareing** aged 7 years One of God's little smiles

*In church*

To the Glory of God and in the memory of **Humphrey Ignatius Watts** of Sion House who died 9<sup>th</sup> February 1949 RIP
This Sanctuary was adorned and embellished by his widow Ethel M Watts in the year of Our Lord 1953.

J7          RIP **Berenice** dear daughter of Lionel and Veronica **Webster**, curators of Harvington Hall, born 1<sup>st</sup> April 1939, died 10<sup>th</sup> September 1954. Ad deum qui laetificat juventum meum, Now also her beloved mother **Veronica Mary Platt Webster** born 5<sup>th</sup> June 1907, died 8<sup>th</sup> July 1992.

J18/19          IHS Of your charity pray for the repose of the soul of **Ann Whitehouse** died September 6<sup>th</sup> 1900 aged 91 years also **Ann Emery** died June 9<sup>th</sup> 1902 aged 84 years. May they rest in peace.

|13          Of your charity pray for the repose of the soul of **John Whitehouse** of Walsall who died at Harvington May 16 1892 aged 68 years. On whose soul Sweet Jesus have mercy RIP

A10/          In loving memory of **Patricia Ann Wilkes** Died 15<sup>th</sup> August 1973 Age 40

A5

F12          Of your charity pray for the repose of the soul of **Eliza**

**Mary Wood** wife of **G T Wood of Dudley** who died Dec 9th 1890 in the 35th year of her age.

Also of the above **George Thomas Wood** who died at Red Cross Chaddesley Corbett April 17th 1929 aged 68 years RIP

B17   IHS Jesus mercy Mary help of your charity pray for the repose of the soul of **Eliza** wife of **G V Wood** of Red Cross, Chaddesley Corbett died March 25th 1900 May she rest in peace.

(G.V. Wood d.1920 also buried here)

A16   Of your charity pray for the repose of the soul of **Margaret Winifred Wood** of Red Cross, Chaddesley Corbett on whose soul Sweet Jesus have mercy. Died 16th Feb 1969 in her 80th year RIP Always remembered by her cousin Pat. Here is also buried **Marjorie Thomas** who died 23 June 2001 aged 91. In loving memory of Marjorie M Thomas nee **Stephens** widow of the late John **Thomas**, 1st Nov 1915–23rd June 2001. At rest with your family the **Hailes** of Harvington.

B20   Of your charity pray for the soul of **William Woodward** 7th 1908 . . . . . . . . 7? W . . . . . . . .

# APPENDIX II
# POST-REFORMATION
# INSCRIPTIONS IN
# ST CASSIAN'S CHURCH

### HUMPHREY PAKINGTON
HEERE LYETH THE BODY OF HVMFREY PAKINGTON ESQ
WHO DEPARTED THIS LIFE THE VIth DAY OF AVGUST 1631
HEE WAS SONNE OF JOHN PAKINGTON OF CHADDESLEY
CORBET
ESQr AND MARRIED ABIGALL DAVGHTER OF HENRY
SACHEVERELL
IN THE COVNTY OF DERBY ESQVIRE BY WHOM HEE HAD
ISSUE
MARY & ANNE. MARY MARRIED Sr JOHN YATE OF BVCK-
LAND IN Ye COVNTY OF BERKE Kt & BARONETT. ANNE
MARRIED SIR
HENRY AVDELEY OF BEERECHURCH IN Ye COVNTY OF
ESSEX Kt
Wch SAIDE ANNE LADY AVDELEY TOGETHER WITH HER
YOVNGEST
SONNE HENRY LYE ALSO NEERE HEERE VNTO INHVMED.
& NEERE AS MAY BEE VNTO THIS PLACE THE SAID
MISTRIS
PAKINGTON (WHOSE COSTE AND CHARGE THIS IS)
INTENDETH
BY THE PERMISSION OF ALMIGHTY GOD TO BE ALSO
INTERRED

In memory of you who did dispise
Vayne, pompe though in yr self both rich & wise
And filde, not swolne with knowledge did possess
The rarest Mixture of all Sciences,
That those who truly studied you might knowe
The truths which best of bookes obscurely shew
Heere I your Loyall wife these Numbers send
To testify that loue which nere shall end
For to your Vertues render it I must
Till I lye Bedded here with you in dust,
From whence I hope wee shall in glory rise
And Farr surmount what's seene by mortall Eyes
And then nor time nor death shall us annoye
But wee shall triumphe in Eternall Ioye

## ABIGAIL PAKINGTON

TWAS PROVIDENCE, PRESERV'D THIS MARBLE HERE
BY WHITE TO SPEAKE, HER CANDOR, AND NOW BEAre
INSCRIB'D THIS EPITAPH, TO VSHER FORTH
HER MANY VERTVES, PRVDENCE, GOODNES, WORTh,
AND – OH! I AM CONFIN'D TO, STRAIGHTS, AND MVST
SMOOTHER THE REST, CONCLVDE, HERE LIED THE DVST
AND WIDOWE RARE, EXEMPLAR IN EACH LIFe
A DERELICT OF SIX AND TWENTY YEARES,
THE SVN MAY BE OBSCUR'D, AND SPANGL'D SPHERES
YET (MAVGRE DEATH) HER FAME CONTINEWES BRIGHt
VERTVE'S A GLOWORME, AND WILL SHINE BY NIGHT
Obijt die 7 Aug.Ao.Dni
1657
Requiescat in pace

## MARY YATE
### DEO OPTIMO MAXIMO

Here lies the Eldest Daughter and coheire of HUMPHREY PACK-
INGTON Esqr Lord of ye Manner of *Chadsley Corbet*, and the
Incomparable Widow of Sr JOHN YATE of *Buckland* Knight and
Baronet; the Lady *MARY YATE*, of pious memory, whose loss is too
great to be forgotten.

She lived for the common good, and died for her own. She lived too well to fear death, and could not have died, if the prayers of the poor had prevailed, her Prudence in ye management of a bad world was allwais aiming at a better. Her justice was more than exact in paying all she owed even before it was due. Her Fortitude was built upon her faith, a rock wch no storm could move, her Temperence was grounded on her Hope & Charity, wch raised her heart so much above ye world, that she used it without enjoying it, she bestowed it liberally upon those who needed it, & left it as easely, as if she had allwaies despised it. Ripe for Heaven and full of Vertues as of daies she died in ye 86th year of her Age the 12th day of June in the year of our Lord 1696 after having been Lady of this manner 63 years.

*Requiescat in Pace*
This is a Dutyfull tribute Erected by her Daughter
APOLONIA YATE


### ANN AUDELEY
IN MEMORY OF DAME ANN AVDELEY LATE WIFE OF
Sr. HENRY AVDELEY OF BEERECHURCH IN THE
COVNTY OF ESSEX KNIGHT AND DAVGHTER OF
HUMFREY PAKINGTON ESQr. & ABIGALL HIS WIFE
THE SAID DAME ANN DEPARTED THIS LIFE THE
23 OF NOVEMBER 1642. LEAVING BEHINDE HER
ONE SONNE & THREE DAVGHTERS TOGETHER
WITH THIS TRVE CHARACTER OF HER GREAT
VERTVES VIZt.

Generous reader staye and you shall here
A truth that's worthy your attentive eare
Know neere this place interred lyes
One that had all those excellent qualities
of Noble vertuous beautifull and wise
A Mortall Creature could immortalize
Shee was exemplar in all pious wayes
vnto her sex wynninge theire highest prayes
and euermore most humbly did aspire
to beare a parte wth th Angells in theire Quire

# APPENDIX III
# DAME MARY YATES'S FINANCIAL SUPPORT FOR THE PRIESTS OF HARVINGTON AND BUCKLAND 1677

THIS INDENTURE tripartite made the first day of May in the twenty ninth year of the Reign of our Sovereign Lord Charles the Second by the grace of God King of England Scotland France & Ireland Defender of the Faith etc Anno Domini 1677 Between Dame Mary Yate of Harvington in the County of Worcester Widow of the first part John Perrott Dean of the Chapter of the English Secular Clergy of the second part and John Belson of Lond: Esqr & Thomas Keightley of Lond: Gentn of the third part Whereas in and by one Indenture bearing even date with these presents made between the same & Dame Mary Yate on the one part and John Belson of London Esqr and Thomas Keightley of Lond: Gent; on the other part It is mentioned that the said Dame Mary Yate hath given granted and confirmed unto the said John Belson and Thomas Keightley and their heirs One annual rent of Fifty pounds of lawful money of England to be issuing out of several Marsh lands lying within Hebunheath Marsh and Poplar Marsh or one of them in the Parish of Hebunheath alias Stepney in the County of Middlesex payable and to be paid yearly on the feast day of the Annunciation of the Blessed Virgin Mary and the feast day of St Michael the Archangel by equal portions at or in the Common Dining Hall of the Middle Temple London the first payment thereof to be made and begin on the first past day of the feast days aforesaid which shall happen next after the day of the death of the same Dame

Mary Yate without any defalcation or abatement for or in respect of taxes or otherwise with a proviso in the same Indenture contained for making void the same upon payment of the principal sum of One thousand pounds of lawful money of Engl$^d$ by the said Dame Mary Yate or by her heirs or assigns unto the said John Belson & Thomas Keightley their heirs executors or assigns at such time and in such manner and with such forfeits as by the said Indenture whereunto this refers more at large appeareth Now this Indenture witnesseth that it is mutually declared by and between all and every the same parties to these presents that the said recited Indenture and the Grant thereby made was so made and granted by the said Dame Mary Yate not for any money or other consideration by her received for the same but voluntarily upon trust to and for the several uses intents & purposes hereafter declared that is to say, that as well the said annual rent of Fifty pounds as the said principal sum of One thousand pounds payable for the redemption thereof, shall from time to time hereafter be had & received by the Dean & Chapter of the English Secular Clergy and their successors for ever Upon trust and to the intent to be by them paid and distributed to two Priests of the said English Secular Clergy in manner following viz 'Twenty five pounds annually to be paid to one of the said Priests who shall reside in or near Chadsley Corbett for the assistance and spiritual help of such poor Catholics in Worcestershire or thereabout as shall be judged most to need such spiritual help by the aforesaid Dean & Chapter and Twenty five pounds annually to be paid to the other of the said Priests who shall reside at or near Buckland in the County of Berks and assist and help such poor Catholics in the said County or thereabout as shall likewise there be judged most to need such spiritual help by the aforesaid Dean & Chapter who shall nominate and appoint the said two priests to the said assistance and help of the poor respectively as aforesaid And it is hereby further declared that in case the Roman Catholic religion shall hereafter be restored & settled in Engl$^d$ that then and from henceforth the several trusts and appointments above mentioned shall cease and determine and in such case as well the annual rent of Fifty pounds as the said principal sum of One thousand pounds shall be disposed & employed towards the Parish Church of Buckland in the County of Berks for the maintenance of an Assistant Priest to the Pastor or Vicar for the time being of the said Church for ever And lastly it is declared that in case the said principal sum shall at any time hereafter be paid in according to the tenor and intent of the proviso or condition of redemption in the above recited Indenture contained that then the said sum shall by and with the consent & approbation of the said Dame Mary Yate and her heirs be disposed and laid out in the purchase of lands or yearly rent or upon security at interest Upon trust to and for the same uses intents and purposes as in and by these presents are before declared and appointed and to and for no other use intent or purpose whatsoever In witness whereof all the said parties have hereunto put their hands and seals the day and year first above written

John (L. S.) Perrott Dean_____Jo. (L. S.) Belson_____
_____Tho: (L. S.) Keightley_____
Sealed and delivered in the presence of Lawrence Jones John Morgan

___

Alexander Holt Secretary of the Chapter.


## MEMORANDUM CONCERNING BUCKLAND & HARVINGTON JULY 6th 1735

An estate in Poplar Marsh, alias the Isle of Dogs, of the value of about £350 per an. now in the hands of Mr (?) Tt (Talbot ?) was engaged to the Dean and Chapter by M$^{rs}$ Ap. Yates, in K. James Reign by an original deed to pay 90 odd pounds to the Professors or Masters of D. College and £50 per an. to Buckland & Harvington. Two thirds of this estate were suggested by B.St$^r$ (Bishop Stonor) to be settled on Lord Widdrington, the other third to be now in M$^r$ T$^{ts}$ (Talbot ?) power. Great charges attend it to secure it against the Thames w$^{ch}$ almost surrounds it, being over against Greenwich joining Blackwall at the end of London, little profit to the present Possessor for some years past – the same lady gave £200 to M$^r$ Green of Harvington for the help of poor Catholics & as B. St.$^r$ could not get the principal from him the said S. agreed that the interest of it, sh$^{ld}$ during Mr Green's life, be for the priest's salary (now M$^r$ – ?) in his house on condition that at his death he should pay £400 to the said Bishop, or his successor, for w$^{ch.}$ Mr Green has given bond – By the original deed, the Dean of the Chapter is the collator to Buckland & Harvington, & therein it is provided that if the presented (priest) is by any means hindered from living in the Manor Houses, in that case they sh$^{ld}$ be as near as maybe, so as to be able to help in the places aforesaid.

Feby 5th 1856

My dear Sir

On the other side is the copy of an old paper I found here, dated July 6 1735 – There is neither address or signature – but it seems to be the history of the Harvington Mission and may interest you & be deposited in its archives.

Truly yrs

R Throckmorton

Buckland

## INDENTURE OF 1686 BETWEEN DAME MARY YATE and SILVESTER JENKS (JENCKS)

**This Indenture** made the Tenth day of February Anno Dom[in]i 1686 And in the Third yeare of the reigne of our Sov[e]raigne Lord James the Second by the grace of God of England Scotland France and Ireland King defender of the faith etc.

*Betweene* Dame Mary Yate of Harvington in the County of Worcester widowe on the one part and Silvester Jencks of Harvington aforesaid gent on the other part *Witnesseth* that the said Dame Mary Yate for and in considerac[i]on the som[m]e of foure hundred and fifty pounds of lawfull money of England to her in hand before thensealeing and deliv[er]y of these pr[e]sents by the said Silvester Jencks well and truely paid whereof shee acknowledgeth the Receipt and thereof and of ev[er]y part and parcell thereof doth acquite release exon[er]ate and discharge the said Silvester Jencks his executors and adm[inistrato]rs by these pr[e]sents *Hath* Given graunted and confirmed and by these pr[e]sents doth give graunt and confirme unto the said Silvester Jencks one Anuity or yearely Rent Charge of five and forty pounds of lawfull money of England to bee issueing payable and goeing out of *All* those messuages lands meadows closes pastures Tenem[en]ts and hereditam[en]ts scituate lyeing and being in the parish of Chaddesley Corbett in or neare a place there called Cakebould in the said County of Worcester heretofore in the sev[er]all tenures of Humfrey Newneham, John Baylis, Edward Jones, Anne Cooke and William Newnham, and nowe in the tenure of the said Dame Mary Yate her underten[a]nt or underten[a]nts the inheritance of all which said messuages lands and Tenem[en]ts shee the said Dame Mary Yate late had and purchased to her and her heires for ever of her Grandchild Mary Yate nowe the wife of S[i]r Robert Throgmorton Baronn[e]t To have hould receive take and enioye the said

Anuity of yearely Rent Charge of five and forty pounds unto the said
Silvester Jencks and his assignes for and dureing the naturall life of
him the said Silvester Jencks to bee paid at the feasts of the Annun-
ciac[i]on of the blessed Lady St Mary the Virgin and the feast of St
Michael tharchAngell by even and equall porc[i]ons at or in the now
manc[i]on house of the said Dame Mary Yate in Harvington aforesaid
The first paym[e]nt thereof to bee made on the feast day of the Annun-
ciac[i]on of the blessed Lady St Mary the Virgin next comeing *And*
the said Dame Mary Yate for her and her heires doth Coven[a]nt and
graunt to and with the said Silvester Jencks that if and as often as it
shall happen the said Anuity or yearely Rent of five and Forty pounds
or any part thereof shall bee behind and unpaid by the space of Fower-
teene dayes next after either of the said feast dayes whereon the same
ought to bee paid as aforesaid being lawfully demanded that then and
soe often shee the said Dame Mary Yate her heires and assignes shall
forfeit and Loose unto the said Silvester Jencks the som[m]e of two
shillings of lawfull money of England noie pene[1] for ev[er]y day the
said Anuity or yearely Rent Charge or any part thereof shall bee soe
behind and unpaid And that then and soe often it shall and may bee
lawfull to and for the said Silvester Jencks and his assignes into all
and singuler the said lands Tenem[en]ts and hereditam[en]ts aforesaid
to enter and distreyne as well for the said Anuity or yearely Rent of
five and Forty pounds and all arrerages thereof if any shall happen as
alsoe for the said Som[m]e of two shillings soe to bee forfeited noie
pene as aforesaid and the distresse and distresses there from time to
time found and taken to beare lead drive take and carry away and the
same to withhould deteyne keepe and impound until aswell of the said
Anuity or yearely Rent Charge of five and forty pounds and all
arrerages thereof if *any* shall happen as the said som[m]e and
som[m]es of money soe to be forfeited noie pene if any shall bee and
all Costs and damages in that behalfe susteyned hee the said Silvester
Jencks and his assignes shall bee fully satisfied contented and paid
*And* the said Mary Yate for herselfe and for her heires and assignes
doth Coven[a]nt to and with the said Silvester Jencks and his assignes
by these pr[e]sents that (for and notwithstanding any Act matter or
thing by her done to the contrary) the said sev[er]all messuages lands
and Tenem[en]ts with their appurten[a]nc[e]s shall bee and contynue
all times chargeable and liable to all and ev[er]y the distresse and
distresses of the said Silvester Jencks and his assignes according to the
purport intent and true meaneing of these pr[e]sents there to bee had
and taken at any time for default of paym[en]t of the said Anuity or

yearely Rent Charge and the said som[m]e and som[m]es of money soe to bee forfeited noie pene as aforesaid or any part thereof *In witness* whereof of the parties first above named to these pr[e]sent Indentures theire hands and seales Interchaingably have put the day and yeare first above written.

[Signed] Marie Yate

[1] nomine pene = approximately

# APPENDIX IV

A

TRUE COPY

OF THE

SPEECH

OF

Mr. *Francis Johnstons*, alias, *Dormore*, alias *Webb*

alias *Wall*;

A PRIEST

of the

𝕮𝖍𝖚𝖗𝖈𝖍 𝖔𝖋 𝕽𝖔𝖒𝖊,

(Who was Convicted before Mr. *Justice Atkins*, at *Worcester*, last *Lent-Assizes*, upon an Indictment on the Statute of the 27 *Eliz*. Cap.2,) Which he spake upon the Ladder, immediately before his Execution, on *Fryday* last, *August* 22. 1679.

With ANIMADVERSIONS upon the same. [omitted here]

Almighty *God*, out of his infinite goodness to this World, through the Merits of his Son *Christ Jesus*, ordained or made choice of Three Vertues, whereby we must walk; which are these, *viz. Faith, Hope*, and *Charity*.
*First*, By the Virtue of faith, we are to believe all things that are done in this World. *Secondly*, By Virtue of Hope, we are to believe and hope for all things in another World: And the Reason why Christians do believe this Hope, is to bring and conduct them to Salvation in the other World. And if we Hope in *God*, we cannot but Believe *God*:

For *with the Mouth, Confession is made; but with the Heart*; (and through *Faith*) *we must believe unto Salvation.* So that *faith* is not to be trodden under Foot, or to be hidden under a Bushel; but to be set upon a Candlestick. *Luke* the 12th. *Whosoever doth confess me before Men, him will I confess before the Angels of God; And him that denies me before Men, him will I deny before the Angels of God.* And therefore, all are bound to believe, that there is but one *Faith*; and if but one *Faith*, then but one *Christian Faith.* There is but one *Faith*, one *Lord*, one *Baptism*: And if it be so, How can this stand with so many Sectaries as there are? And if there be one *Faith*, How can this be?

I believe the Creed of St. *Athanasius*, (which is in your *Common Prayer-Book*) and there it is said, *That whosoever will be saved, tis necessary before all things, that he hold the* Catholick-Faith; *and that if he keep not that* Faith *whole and undefiled, he shall perish everlastingly.* And as St. *James* saith, (*Jam.* 2. 10) *He that keepeth the whole Law, and yet offendeth in one Point, is guilty of All*: So they that believe, must be all of the same *Faith.* And that this ought to be done, I do appeal to all the Saints that are gone before; of whom it is said, *Heb.* 11. *That their* Faith *was such, as by it they stopt the Mouths of Lyons, they turned the Edge of the Sword, and caused the Fire to cease, that it should not burn*: And *They were opressed so, they wandered about in Sheep Cloathing, and Goats Cloathing.* Therefore, I say, there must be an Unity of Faith.

I desire all *Catholicks* to consider this, That it is better to be Reviled by Man now in this World, than to be Reviled by God in the World to come. *Matth.* 16. its said, *The Catholick Church is built upon a Rock*: And *Matth.* 18. *He who will not believe the Church, let him be as a Heathen and a Publican.* This *Faith* must be Establisht so in every one, because *Christ* said, *He would send the Holy Ghost, and he shall show us* (or them) *what to do.*

This is the Rule of *Faith*: This *Faith* was publisht at *Rome*: and St. *Paul* writing to the Christians there, Rejoyceth that their Faith was Renowned in the Whole World. *Go ye therefore, Baptizing all Nations in the Name of the Father.* And this is the *Faith* which I confess and Believe in, and which I dy for.

I come now to speak of the second Vertue, which is *Hope.* I Hope, I shall have such Reward, *that neither Eye hath seen, not Ear heard, nor can it enter into the Heart of man to conceive.*

Those that have *Hope*, shall be as *Mount Zion*, that shall not be

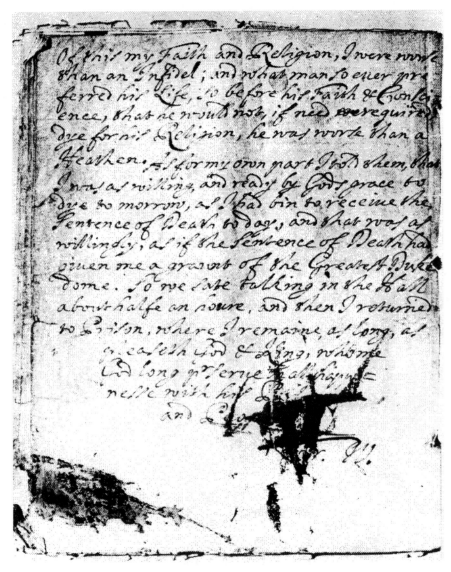

St John Wall's autographed account of his last days.

Removed: Those that have *Firm Hope*, there is nothing can disturb them; because *David* saith. *That* God *is round about His, that do hope in Him, as the Mountains are round about* Jerusalem.

I come to the Third Virtue and that is *Charity*. It's true, now this Body of mine in this Shipwrack is full of Sin; but when that Shipwrack is over, I shall come to inherit that *Rock*, that shall never fail. Now, wellcom Shipwrack, that makes the Body suffer, but brings the Soul to that Haven which is Joyful. Now many there be, that talk much of *Charity*, few understand it, and fewer that practice it. This is the greatest Virtue. 1 *Cor.* 13. *Though you speak with the Tongues of men and Angels, and have not Charity, it availeth nothing.* So then, we ought to have *Love and Charity*, or else it prevaileth nothing.

Tis Expected I should say something of the Plot: as to this, I shall declare two points of my faith.

*First*, I believe, that all are bound to obey the King and his Laws.

*Secondly*, I do declare, that those that do break the Law in Word, or any Action, that doth Act anything against his Majesties Life, that it is a sin unto damnation, as much as it was a sin in *Judas* to betray Christ. An Oath, is taking God to Witness; and is as much as if he took his Life and Justice to stake; so that he that takes a false Oath, is guilty of destroying the Life of God, and his Justice, and of his own Damnation: And if I were but Guilty of this, I do declare, that all the sin of Damnation would fall upon me, because I denied the truth, and so struck at God by my sin, by denying of the Truth, that one Damnation.

A Second Damnation is, that if any man know of an evil against his Majesty, his Kingdome and nation, and to hide, or not discover it, he shall Answer for those Mischiefs that come thereby: so that a man would have made and Committed as many sins as there are men in *England*, that had suffered:

A Third Damnation is, to die in this Lie, and with this perjury in his mouth: that he loses Heaven and all the enjoyments, and dies in greater sins than the Devils themselves.

*Fourthly*, I should have been Guilty of my own death, for that Justice *Atkins* offered me my Life, if I would confess what I knew of the Plot; which had I known, and not discovered, would have made me the Cause of my own death, which would have been a fourth Damnation.

I would have said more, but that I gave my speech to a friend to be printed.

Mr. *Sherif*, I Pray Sir, speak on what you have to say, and no one shall interrupt you.

Mr. *Johnston*. Now I have no more to do, but to make my address to Almighty God will all the powers of my soul, that I may have his mercy and pardon of my sins; and therefore I beg, that all the Catholicks that joyn in union of this same Faith, would make ann address unto God for me, that we may receive pardon for our Sins: I have nothing now, but wishes left;

I wish I may Imitate David in his Repentance, and that *My Eyes may run down with Tears, because I have not kept God's Laws.* I wish with the prophet *Jeremiah*, that *Rivers of waters may fall from my Eyes, by reason of sin*, Lam. 3. 48. But tears will not be proper to me at this time, I have kept my self from them, lest by shedding Tears, some might say, I was unwilling to die, or feared death: but instead of Tears, I offer all the Blood in my veins; and I wish every drop were an Ocean, and I would offer it up unto God; and I wish, that I might become a man like *David*, I wish I had *Mary Magdalens* penitential Tears; I wish I had her Arms to embrace the feet of mercy; I wish I had all the Graces of Saints and Angels, and I would offer them all to God for the Remission of my sin: this is my desire, and this I wish for, as much as is in me.

I offer first my Life, and I beseech and desire of God, to turn his face from my sins, but not from me. I offer up my Life in satisfaction for my sins, and for the Catholick Cause: and I beg for those that be my Enemies in this my death, and I desire to have them forgiven, because I go to that World of Happiness, sooner than I should have gone. And humbly beg pardon from God and the World; And this I beg for the Merits and Mercy of *Jesus Christ*. I beseech *God* to bless his Majesty; and give him a long Life, and Happy Reign in this World, and in the World to come. I beseech God to bless all my Benefactors, and all my Friends, and those that have been any way under my charge. I beseech God to bless all the Catholicks, and this Nation, and his Majesties privy Council; and grant that they may Act no otherwise, than what may be for the Glory of God, *Luk. 12. who will bring to light and to Judgement all, both good and evil.*

So I beseech God, that he will give them Grace to serve him

I beseech God to Bless the Parliament that is now in Election, that they may determine nothing, but what they themselves do hope to be Judged by at the last day.

I beseech *God* to bless all that suffer under this Persecution, and to turn this our Captivity into Joy; that they which Sow now in Tears, may Reap in Joy.

I beseech *God* to save the Death of my Body, and to receive my Soul, I have no more to say.

Mr. *Sheriff.* I give you no Interruption, but only whereas you said, *That you Dyed for the Faith*; that is not so: You do not Dye for that; but because you being his Majesties Subject, received Orders from the *Church of Rome*, beyond the Seas; and came again into *England*, contrary to the Law.

Mr. *Johnst.* That was pardoned by the King's Act of Grace.

Mr. *Sher.* That Act pardoned only Crimes committed before the making of it; but not-those done since, as your Continuance in *England* was.

Mr. *Johnst.* I am sorry, if I have given Offence in anything I have said: My Reason for it was, because when I was sent for to the Judges upon *Sunday*-Night, Judge *Atkins* told me, *I Dyed not for being concerned in the Plot, but for being a Priest.*

Mr. Sher. No, but for your Continuance in *England* against the Law, (being a Priest.)

Mr. *Johnst. God* receive my Soul

Mr. *Sher.* Sir, You may take your own time, and you shall have no Interruption Sir, Will you be pleased to have your own time.

*Jaylor* Sir, Pray give the Signe, when you please to be Turned Off

Mr. *Johnst.* I will give you no Signe; Do it when you will

    *(And he was Executed.)*

# SOURCES AND BIBLIOGRAPHY

a.　Original source material

Birmingham Archdiocese Archives
Harvington Parish Archives
Harvington Hall Archives
Worcestershire County Records

b.　Secondary sources

Archdiocese of Birmingham Yearbooks, Obituaries
Catholic Directory
Catholic Miscellany
Catholic Record Society and Occasional Publications
Midland Catholic History
Staffordshire Recusant
The Tablet
Worcestershire Recusant

Anstruther, Geoffrey, O.P., *The Seminary Priests*, vols.1–4, Mayhew McCrimon, Great Wakering, 1968–1977.

Bauer, Petra, 'Roman Catholic Elementary Education in Victorian England', Course-paper for Victorian Studies M. Litt., Social History 1988.

Bossy, John, *The English Catholic Community 1570–1850*, Darton, Longman and Todd, London, 1975.

Camm, Dom Bede, O.S.B., *Forgotten Shrines*, Macdonald and Evans, London 1910, reprinted, Gracewing, Leominster, 2004.

Caraman, Philip, S.J., *Henry Garnet and the Gunpowder Plot*, Longmans, London, 1964.

Dodd, Charles, D.D, *The Church History of England, 1500 to 1688*, 1–3 vols, Brussels, 1737.

Dodd, Charles, D.D., *The Secret Policy of the English Society of Jesus*, London, 1715.

Fea, Alan, *Secret Chambers and Hiding Places*, Bousfield and Co., London, 1904.

Gillow, Joseph, *Biographical Dictionary of the English Catholics*, 5 vols, Burns & Oates, London, 1909.

Gooch, Leo (ed.), *The Revival of English Catholicism, The Bannister-Rutter Correspondence, 1777–1807*, North West Catholic History Society, Wigan, 1995.

Hemmingway, Vincent, *Coughton Court and the Throckmortons*, Coughton Court and Harrold Publishing, 1993.

Hemphill, Dom Basil, O.S.B., *The Early Vicars Apostolic, 1685–1750*, Burns & Oates, London, 1954.

Hodgetts, Michael, *Harvington Hall*, Archdiocese of Birmingham Historical Commission, 1998.

Hodgetts, Michael, *Harvington 1200–2000*, Archdiocese of Birmingham Historical Commission, 2002.

Hodgetts, Michael, *St Joseph's, Upton-upon-Severn, 1850–2000*.

Hodgetts, Michael, *Secret Hiding Places*, Oscott Series 3, 1989.

Kelly, Bernard, *Historical Notes on English Catholic Missions*, Kegan Paul, London, 1907.

Kirk, John, D.D., *Biographies of English Catholics in the 18th century*, Pollen and Burton (eds), Burns & Oates, London, 1909.

Palmer, R. A., *St Cassian's, Chaddesley Corbett, before and after the restoration of 1863/4*, 1994.

Panzani, Gregorio, *The Memoirs*, trans. by Dodd with introduction and supplement by the Revd Joseph Berington, Birmingham, 1793, introduction by T. A. Birrell. Gregg International Press, 1970.

Pevsner, N., *Worcestershire*, Penguin, 1968.

Pullen, G. F., Recusant Books at St. Mary's, Oscott, Parts I and II, Oscott, 1964.

Roper, John, *A History of St Cassian's, Chaddesley Corbett*, 1978.

Sergeant, John, *An Account of the Chapter erected by William, titular Bishop of Chalcedon and Ordinary of England and Scotland*, James Darling, London, 1853.

Squiers, Granville, *Secret Hiding Places*, Stanley Paul, 1933.

Tangye, Elizabeth, *The Families and Village of Chaddesley Corbett in the 19th century*, Chaddesley Corbett Local History Group, 1995.

Tierney, M. A., *Dodd's Church History* with notes, additions and a continuation. 5 vols, London, 1839.

Walker, R. O., *Hartlebury*, A record of the parish.

Ward, Bernard, *The Eve of Catholic Emanicipation*, 3 vols, Longmans, 1911.

# BIBLIOGRAPHY OF THE
# HARVINGTON PRIESTS

JENKS, Silvester

1 *Theses ex Theologia Universa. Praeside Reverendo Domino Eduardo Paston, Sacrae Theologiae Professore, tueri conabitur in aula Collegii Anglorum Duaceni. Silvester Jenksius, Die iv. Id.* Jul. 1680. Duaci, 1680, 4to., with dedicatory preface to Guida de Save, bishop of Arras.

2 *A letter concerning the Council of Trent.* By N N 1686, 24mo pp. 264.

3 *A Sermon preached before the King at Windsor*, Aug 24 1687, London, 1687, 4to.

4 *A Sermon preached before the King at Whitehall*, June 14 1688, London, 1688, 4to.

5 *A Sermon preached before their Majesties at Windsor*, Aug 26 1688, London, 4to.

6 *A Contrite and Humble Heart: with Motives and Considerations to prepare it*, Paris, 1692, 12mo London, T. Meighan, 1698, 12mo.

7 *Practical Discourses upon the Morality of the Gospel. In two parts*, 1699, 24mo p. 224, London, T. Meighan, 1817, 8vo.

8 *The Blind Obedience of a Humble Penitent, the best cure for Scruples*, 1699, 12mo., republished under the title *God's Safe Way of Obedience* revised and edited by a priest (the Rev Charles Bowen) London, 1872, 12mo pp. 138.

9   *The Security of an Humble Penitent, in a letter to H S 1700*, 12mo.

10   *The Whole Duty of a Christian. In Three Parts, etc., being a Faithful Abstract of the Trent Catechism, etc. 1707*, 12mo.

11   *An Essay upon the Art of Love.*

12   *An Essay on the Art of Love*, abridged.

13   *A Discourse of Submission to the Powers in being.* MS.

14   *A Short review of the Book of Jansensius. 1710*, 12mo.

15   *Letters concerning Jansenism.* MS, 8vo pp. 29, Ushaw Coll. MSS, I. f. 353.

TOOTELL, Hugh (alias CHARLES DODD)

1   *The History of the English College at Douay*, London, Bern, Lintott, 1713, 8vo.

2   *The Secret Policy of the English Society of Jesus*, London, Jno. Morphew, 1715, 8vo.

3   *The Free Man, or Loyal Papist*, MS, fragments of which are printed in the *Catholicon*, 1817, iv. 161, 275.

4   *The Dissenters' Claim to Places of Trust justified.* MS, 4to.

5   *A Treatise on Providential Allegiance.* MS, 4to.

6   *An Historical Essay in favour of Providential Allegiance*, MS, 4to. temp. Eliz., at Oscott.

7   *A Theological Essay in Favour of Providential Allegiance.* MS, 4to.

8   *General Claim or Allegiance*, MS, 4to.
A work was published by 'P R' in 1716, entitled – 'Doctor utriusque Juris: a Roman Catholic System of Allegiance in favour of the present Establishment', very similar in plan and reasoning

to the above four, and probably by Tootell.

9 *Remarks On Hoadley's 'Preservative against the Principles and Practices of the Non-jurors'*, MS, 4to probably printed. Hoadley, Bishop of Bangor, published his work in 1716, and Dr Thomas Sherlock, subsequently, Bishop of London, published *A Vindication of the Corporation and Test Acts; in answer to the Bishop of Bangor's Reasons for the Repeal of them, 1718*, Tootell followed with–

10 *An Answer to Dr Sherlock's Vindication of the Corporation and Test Acts*, MS, 4to pp. 22, probably printed.

11 *An Answer to the Rev Wm Law's First and Second Letters to the Bishop of Bangor*, MS, 4to pp. 48, probably printed, elicited by 'The Bishop of Bangor's late Sermon, and his Letter to Dr Snape in defence of it, answered', by the Rev Wm Law MA.

12 *Remarks on Dr Fiddes' Divinity*. MS, 4to. Dr Richard Fiddes published *Theologia Speculativa; or a body of Divinity*, 1718–20, 2 vols.

13 *Pax Vobis. An Epistle to the Three Churches; with an Addition of a Preface and Postscript; setting forth the Rule for the Truth and true sense of Scriptures*, London, 1721, 8vo, title and pref. 4ff. pp. 3–135 (preface and postscript were added). Written in opposition to Dr Hoadley, and forming part of the famous Bangorian Controversy.

14 *A Disclaimer of Popish Orders. On Non-jurors*, MS, 4to part of the Bangorian Controversy, and probably printed.

15 *Certamen Utriusq; Ecclesiae: or, A List of all the Eminent Writers of Controversy, Catholicks and Protestants, since the Reformation. With an Historical Idea of the Politick Attempts of both Parties in every Reign* ......
*By Charles Dodd S. 1. 1724*, 4to p. 17.

16 *Catholic Remains; or, A Catholic History of the Reformation in England, Part I*. MS, fol. 99. 191.

17  *Catholic Remains; or, The Lives of English Catholic Clergy, Regulars, and Laymen, from 1500, Part. II.* MS, fol. p. 748, at Oscott.

18  *Annals of Henry VIII, James I. and Charles II*, MS, 8vo.

19  *Annals of the Heptarchy, Normans, etc*, S. I. et a., 4to in print.

20  *Annals of the Reigns of Henry VIII., etc*, S. 1. et a., 4to in print.

21  *Compendium Historicum Ecclesiae in Anglia ab anno 1550*, MSS, 2 vols. 4to i. pp. 336, ii., extending to A. D. 1707, thick sm. 4to. Vol. ii. in old Chapter archives.

22  *History of the Reformation down to George I. in 21 Books*, MS, 4to pp. 292.

23  *Retractions of Bishop Burnet*, MS, 4to.

24  *Remarks on Bishop Burnet's Romance called History of his own Time*, MS, 4to. Burnet's work was published in 1724–34.

25  *Remarks on Dr Conyers Middleton's Letter from Rome*, MS, fol. pp. 22. With reference to Middleton's *A Letter from Rome showing an exact Conformity between Popery and Paganism, 1729*.

26  *Atheists denying a Deity*, MS, 4to.

27  *A Confutation of the Latitudinarian System*, J. Gother, MS, fol., edited and prepared for the press with the addition of a preface and notes.

28  *The Sincere Christian's Guide in the Choice of Religion.* J. Gother, London, Thos Meighan, 1734, 12mo, title and pref. 4ff., p. 196, a posthumous work of the author, edited by Tootell, who wrote the preface.

29  *An Abridgment of Christian Doctrine, with an easy Explanation of the Creed, Commandments, Sacraments, etc.* MS, 4to pp. 30,

printed, and passed through several editions.

30  *A Complete Abridgment of Divinity,* MS, 4to pp. 79.

31  *Historical Account of Visions, Prophesies, etc,* MS, 4to.

32  *Catechistical Instructions on the Creed, Decalogue, etc.* MS, 4to.

33  *The Creed, Lord's Prayer. Commandments, and Sacraments explained,* MS, 4to pp. 238.

34  *Gospels of all the Sundays of the Year, with short Reflections, Moral and Controversial,* MS, 8vo at Oscott.

35  *Christian Instructions, general and particular, delivered in eighty Discourses, methodized by way of Sermons,* MS, fol., pp. 370, at Oscott.

36  *A Treatise of three short Catechisms; first, for new Converts; secondly, for illiterate Persons; and 3rdly, for young Communicants,* MS, 4to pp. 16.

37  *Lives of Penitents in the Deserts, and of other Saints,* MS, 4to.

38  *Authors Unmasked, Rejected, and Vindicated,* MS, 4to.

39  *Controversial Collections,* MS, thick 4to.

40  *The Layman's Manual of Controversy,* MS, 4to.

41  *Controversial Gleanings in Verse, from various Authors,* MS, 8vo.

42  *Controversial Letters,* MS, 8vo.

43  *Catholic Proofs and Protestant Objections,* MS, fol.

44  *A Polemical Dictionary,* MS, 4to pp. 176

45  *A Philosophical and Theological Dictionary,* MS, in 44 nos.

46 *The Protestant Expostulator*, MS, pp. 32.

47 *Barrier between Church and State* MS, 4to pp. 31.

48 *An English Historical, Geographical and Ecclesiastical Dictionary, down to the Reformation*, MS, fol., pp. 278.

49 *Memoirs of Windebank, Secretary of State*, MS, 4to, prepared for the Press, drawn from a translation procured at Rome for Dodd by Bishop Witham, of the 'Relazione della stato della Religione Cattolica in Inghilterra, data alla Santila di N S Urbano VIII. da Gregorio Panzani'. Dodd's translation, entitled *Memoirs of Panzani*, is much abridged, but it is otherwise faithful.

50 *The Principles and Practices of the Court of Rome pleading for the present Establishment of Government*, MS, 4to.

51 *The Consecrators of Parker not true Bishops*, MS, 8vo.

52 *The Dissertation on Protestant Ordination*, MS, large fol., pp. 78.

53 *Historical Catechism of the State of Religion in England*, MS, 4to.

54 *The Origin and Change of Governments in England*, MS, 4to.

55 *Introductory History*, MS, fol. pp. 157, only coming down to the year 600, being the first form and draft of his Church History.

56 *Materials for the Biography of English Catholics*, MS, thick fol.

57 *An Historical and Critical Dictionary, comprising the Lives of the most eminent Roman Catholics, from the year 1500 to 1688*, MS, large fol., 3 vols, in all 1280 pp. The biographies are fuller than those in the printed *History*.

58 *A Brief Chronology of Men's Lives and Actions*, MS, 4to.

59 *Dictionarium Etymologicum undecim Linguorum*, MS, 8vo.

60 *A Description of a large floating Island by Captain Wrangle*, MS, 4to pp. 31.

61 *Life of Dr Oliver Buckeridge, Vicar of Bray*, MS, 4to.

62 *The Humours*, MS, 8vo.

63 *Flores Cleri Anglo-Catholici, or, An Account of All the Eminent Clergymen, who, by their Virtue, Learning and Deaths, have supported the cause of the Church of Rome in England since 1500*, S. 1. et a., 4to p. 16. This was published some time before the *History* as a specimen he says, 'to awaken all persons of curiosity, who are willing to favour the undertaking which is now ready for the Press.'

64 *The Church History of England, from . . . 1500, to . . . 1688*, Brussels (Wolverhampton, pr.) 3 vols, fol., i. 1737, pp. xx–5789, Index pp. 9, ii.1739. p. 526, Index, p. 4 and errata 1 f., iii.,1742, p. 535, Index 2 ff., new edition 1839–43 by Tierney.

65 *An Apology for the Church History of England, from 1500 till 1688.*
Printed in the year 1737. (A reply to Fr John Constable's 'quarrelsome Libel', *A Specimen of Amendments* published under the fictitious name of Clerophilos Alethes.) S.1., 1742, 8vo pp. xv–208.

BISHOP, George

1 *Moral Philosophy: in which a true idea is given of our Summum Bonum, and of all virtues, Theological and Moral . . .* MS of 28 chapters.

2 Lambert's *Maniere d'instruire les pauvres de la Compagne.* Translated into English. MS at Longbirch in 1800.

3 Fr Mannock's *Poor-Man's Catechism*, 1752. Published by Bishop with a preface.

4 Fr Mannock's *Poor-Man's Controversy*, MS prepared for publication.

VAUGHAN, Arthur

1  *The Triumphs of the Cross; or Penitent of Egypt*, in 8 books. Birmingham, 1776, 8vo, pp. xvi–277, founded on the story of Zozim and Mary of Egypt.

2  *The Ghost of Sansom Fields*, S.1.et a., 8vo, written on this occasion of the apostacy of Fr Charles Wharton, S.J., and his leaving the chapel of Sansom Fields, Worcester, in 1782.

3  *Madan's Thelypthora burlesqued*, MS.


BROWNLOW, John

1  *Liberty of Conscience; or a Dialogue between a Catholic Priest and his separated Brethren, to Explain the Nature and Make Known the Worth of Religious Liberty*. London, *c*.1826. Reprinted in David G. Mullan (ed.), *Religious Pluralism in the West: An Anthology*, Blackwell, Oxford, 1998.

2  *History of Chaddesley Corbett and Harvington*, MS, 1 vol., pp. 140, 1855, at Coughton.

3  *Genealogy of the Throckmorton Family*, 3 vols; Genealogy I, pp. 1–399 consists of mediaeval genealogy, heraldry, drawings of tombs etc. Genealogy II, pp. 400–781 consists of similar material for the Tudor, Stuart and Georgian periods, with an index to both vols. Genealogy III consists mostly of abstracts in chronological order of 1,075 Throckmorton deeds from 1281–1681, pp. 89–323 and the index pp. 325–330. But is also contains miscellaneous items mostly relating to the Throckmortons and Harvington. MS now at Coughton, 1857–9.

4  'Memoirs of Harvington Hall', MS, 1859. An article published in *The Cabinet* (not traced) for February 1859 and surviving in MS as pp. 49–72 of Brownlow's *Genealogy of the Throckmorton Family* III.

5  'A Memoir of Harvington Hall', 1872. This brief account, subtitled 'Facts and Probabilities' is not the same as the foregoing *Cabinet* article. A copy is now at the Hall.

6 *Poems*, printed in a very limited edition of only 40, Thomas Mark, Kidderminster, 1860. HPA.

7 'Memoranda Culled from Various Sources, March–April 1874', MS HPA.

CRICHTON, James Dunlop

1 *The Church's worship considerations on the Liturgical Constitution of the Second Vatican Council*, Geoffrey Chapman, London, 1964. x, 246pp., bibliog.

2 *Changes in the liturgy: considerations on the instruction of the Sacred Congregation of Rites for the right ordering and execution of the constitution on the Sacred liturgy issued Rome 26 September 1964*, Geoffrey Chapman, London, 1965, viii, 119pp.
*The parish in the modern world*, Sheed and Ward, 1965. vi, 146p. Contributors: James D Crichton, Michael Gaine, John Fitzsimmons, Charles Davis, Leonard Johnston, Clifford Howell, S.J., and Edward Mitchinson.

3 ed. *The Mass and the people of God*, Burns and Oates, London, 1966. 157pp. (Compass Book).

ed. *The liturgy and the future*, Tenbury Wells, Fowler Wright Books, 1966. 173pp.

4 *Companion to the new order of baptism*, Birmingham and Dublin, Goodliffe Neale, 1970. 240pp.

5 *Christian celebration: the Mass*, Geoffrey Chapman, London, 1971. viii, ii, 196pp.

6 *Christian celebration: the sacraments*, Geoffrey Chapman, London, 1973. xiv, 240pp.

7 *The ministry of reconciliation: a commentary on the order of penance,* Geoffrey Chapman, London, 1974, viii, 167pp. Contains the Ordo Paenitentiae tr into English by Geoffrey Webb.

8 *Christian celebration: the prayer of the Church*, Geoffrey Chapman, London, 1976. x, 134pp.

9 *The once and the future liturgy*, Dublin, Veritas, 1977. 134pp.

10 *The care of the sick*, Catholic Truth Society, London, 1978. 56pp.

11 J. D. Crichton and others, (eds), *English Catholic Worship; liturgical renewal in England since 1900*, ed by J. D. Crichton, H. E. Winstone and J. R. Ainslie (eds), Geoffrey Chapman, London, 1979. xii, 163pp.

12 *Christian celebration: the sacraments*, Geoffrey Chapman, 1980, xiv. 240pp.

   *Praying and Singing*, Collins, London, 1980, 128pp.

13 *Christian celebration; The Mass, The Sacraments, The Prayer of the Church*, 3 volumes in 1. Geoffrey Chapman, London, London, 1981. xiii, 186pp. xi. 270pp. viii, 1349.

14 *A short history of the Mass*, Catholic Truth Society, London, 1983. vi, 75pp., bibliog.

15 J. D. Crichton, (ed.), *Breaking the ice: by those who were lonely but are no longer*, Lewes, Sussex, Temple House Books, 1986. viii, 187pp., bibliog.

16 *Worship in a hidden church*, Blackrock, Dublin, Columba Press, 1988. vi, 134pp., bibliog. *The living Christ: 'In Christ' through Scripture and liturgy*, Collins, London, 1988. ix, 113pp. *Journey through Lent*, Mayhew, 1989.

17 The story of a parish – Holy Redeemer, Pershore 75 years 1913–1988, 1989. *The Coming of the Lord*, Twenty-third publication pp. 88, 1990 –

18 *Servants of the people: today's priest in the light of the second Vatican Council*, Slough, St Paul Publications, 1990. viii, 164pp., *The Dedication of a Church*, Dublin, Veritas Publications, pp. 120, 1964–1990.

19 *The Lord is risen; the liturgy from Passiontide to Pentecost*, Kevin Mayhew, Ltd Bury St Edmunds, 1992, 215pp.

20 *Christian celebration: the Mass*, Geoffrey Chapman, London, 1993. viii, 232pp.

   *Christian celebration: the prayer of the church*, Geoffrey Chapman, London, 1993. x, 165pp.

21 *Celebrating the word: homilies for the Sundays of the year, cycles A, B and C, with introductions on the nature of the liturgical homily, its preparation and its delivery*, Dublin, Columba Press, 1995. 284pp.

22 *Lights in darkness: forerunners of the liturgical movement*, Dublin, Columba Press, 1996. 176pp.

23 *Our Lady in the liturgy*, Dublin, Columba Press, 1997, 110pp.

24 *Preparing for Christmas*, Dublin, Columba Press, 1998, 82pp.

25 *Saints or Sinners? Jansenism and Jansenists in 17th-century France*, Dublin, Veritas Publications, 1999 pp. 288. *As it was – Reminiscences and Prophecies*, Decani, 1999.